CHARLES
SHELDON

Author of *In His Steps*

Ellen Caughey

PUBLISHING, INC.
Uhrichsville, Ohio

Other books in the "Heroes of the Faith" series:

Brother Andrew
Gladys Aylward
William and Catherine Booth
John Bunyan
William Carey
Amy Carmichael
George Washington Carver
Fanny Crosby
Frederick Douglass
Jonathan Edwards
Jim Elliot
Charles Finney
Billy Graham
C. S. Lewis
Eric Liddell
David Livingstone
Martin Luther
D. L. Moody

Samuel Morris
George Müller
Watchman Nee
John Newton
Florence Nightingale
Luis Palau
Francis and Edith Schaeffer
Mary Slessor
Charles Spurgeon
John and Betty Stam
Hudson Taylor
William Tyndale
Corrie ten Boom
Mother Teresa
Sojourner Truth
John Wesley
George Whitefield

ISBN 1-57748-833-4

Published by Barbour Publishing, Inc., P.O. Box 719, Uhrichsville, OH 44683
http://www.barbourbooks.com

Cover illustration © Dick Bobnick.

Member of the
Evangelical Christian
Publishers Association

Printed in the United States of America.

CHARLES SHELDON

one

Topeka, Kansas, January 1946

He had to be careful walking outside in this weather. Patches of snow and ice covered the narrow sidewalk from the house to his backyard study, and he gave each hazardous-looking area his utmost attention. The last thing he wanted was to be laid up in some hospital bed.

In less than a month Charles Monroe Sheldon would turn eighty-nine years old. Although he was in good health—many would say robust—there was no time to waste, and there was no time like the present. Even so, he could feel eyes watching him from the house. If he turned around, he knew he would see the curtains parted on the back door window, the face of his wife, May, peering out. Or perhaps trying to peer outside, her fingers rubbing the frosted glass furiously for a better view. If May were anything, the aged pastor thought with a chuckle, she was stubborn. She would stand guard until he reached his destination.

The "brown study," as parishioners, family, and neighbors called it, loomed just ahead. It was a Spartan structure, no larger than a one-car garage built to accommodate a Model T. While brown lap siding had given the structure its name, its sole occupant had bestowed upon it uncharacteristic renown.

As he entered, Sheldon carefully removed his overcoat and galoshes. A large man, now only slightly stooped from his once regal six-foot frame, he was immaculately dressed. As usual, he wore a three-piece suit. A crisp white handkerchief peeked out from his jacket pocket. In a typical gesture, he smoothed his bald pate before donning spectacles and settling himself at his oak desk to begin the day's work. His well-defined chin jutting upward, he had the look of one who is content for the moment. Charles Sheldon would not be disturbed in the brown study. He expected no calls and would receive none: There was no telephone.

On top of the desk was a typewriter, seemingly pushed away for the moment, and papers. Neatly stacked in one pile were the usual letters to be answered, a task he relished. In another pile were the beginnings of sermons that he might be asked to give. A smile came to his broad face as he recalled those few times every year when his very appearance in the pulpit caused standing-room-only confusion, the kind experienced otherwise only on Christmas Eve or Easter. Back to business, he directed his attention to still another stack of papers that contained the first pages of what might become short stories, and possibly a novel.

Resting atop each pile like a paperweight was a newly polished rock of amber. Shortly after his retirement from the Central Congregational Church of Topeka—for the second and final time, he reminded himself—he had taken up rock collecting and polishing. He enjoyed the feel of the rocks and their beauty. Indeed, many in Topeka prized his collection of amber. But as a hobby (that detestable word, he almost spat it out), rocks could not compare with words. And words, at least words about Jesus, were everything to him.

Fifty years ago he had written the book that had defined his life, and people still sent him letters about it. Why was it so intriguing to wonder what Jesus would do if He were faced with the issues of everyday life? Why, indeed, he thought ironically. That was what roused him from his bed each day, what propelled him into the brown study, what gave him hope and a desire to live. He didn't want to be thought of as some "silver saint" or pastor emeritus. Charles Monroe Sheldon could still write about living as Jesus would want. Eighty-eight years of living was no obstacle to walking in His steps.

Lately, he had received many requests for copies of an article he had written more than twenty years earlier. Perhaps it was fitting that folks would ask him for "Two Old Friends: Old Age and Death," a story that had once appeared in *Christian Herald*. So familiar was he with the text that he could recite the first two sentences from memory:

> *Next to the word "Love," the word "Friend" stands resplendent in human experience. In a world of sordid and self-seeking ambitions, it is a source of mighty satisfaction to know that there is one thing that cannot be bought with money nor won by power.*

The story went on to describe the joys of those golden years if one can only regard old age and death as friends. Did he really believe what he had written now that he found himself on the threshold of heaven? He recalled one of the final sentences of his essay: "But if Old Age shall be a mellow and gracious ripening rather than a rotting, even then Death shall not be a terror, but an anticipation of a new experience that shall be free from the disappointments and distresses of the earthly existence and the promise of an astonishing future."

Rubbing his neatly trimmed white mustache, he glanced around the room. It had been May's idea to have his honorary degrees decorate the walls. There were doctor of divinity degrees from Temple College, nearby Washburn College (where he had been asked to serve as president years ago, an invitation he declined), and his beloved alma mater Brown University. But perhaps his favorite was his honorary doctor of letters degree from Yankton College, Yankton, South Dakota, near where he had spent his youth.

Hardly a day went by that he didn't think about Yankton. Now there was a place where money and power didn't mean too much, Sheldon mused, and where friends and family meant everything. He removed his glasses and rubbed his eyes with large, capable hands. Outside he could hear the whistling of the winter wind, an icy locomotive that would not be derailed from its route.

Now that he had the time to reminisce, he was aware that the years had not dimmed his memory of a time and place where every day was different and exciting. Where he had learned the dignity and value of hard work.

Yes, it was on the wide and silent prairie where he had learned those lessons of life that can be mastered only by having endured adversity. It was on the wide and silent prairie where he first had learned to walk in His steps.

two

Yankton, Dakota Territory, spring 1869

B lue mud, Father! It's all over my hands!" twelve-year-old Charlie shouted down the fifty-five-foot hole in the ground.

"That's good, son. Now why don't you or your brother run and get your mother and sisters? I'm sure they won't want to miss this."

Charlie and his older brother, Ward, turned to each other in amazement. Father had been digging, with their help, of course, for hours, but he sounded like a man who had done a few light chores. Although his clothes were soaked through with sweat and covered with mud, the older man's face bore no evidence of the strain of intense physical labor.

Running to the family's simple log cabin, Charlie was met by the Sheldon women, who were at that moment coming down the porch steps. Alice, the oldest girl and the next oldest child after Charlie, her light brown braids flying in the wind, was carrying a bottle with a rope around its neck.

"For my first taste of homemade water!" she announced grandly.

"Ward and I should get that honor," Charlie shot back. "I haven't seen you make any trips to the river in the last two years!"

Their mother quickly stepped between the two headstrong children, her starched apron rustling against them. "We're all going to benefit from this well. And Alice, we should thank Charlie and Ward for diligently making the four-mile trip all this time."

At the well, Ward was emptying bucket after bucket filled with blue mud sent up from below by his father. After emptying each load, he would then send the bucket, held by ropes and a pulley, down the muddy shaft again. On the last trip down, Ward had placed Alice's glass bottle inside the bucket.

After making a special effort to dig a little deeper for drinkable water, Father was the first to quench his thirst. "It's all right," he announced. "There's no alkali taste. It's good and sweet." In a few moments the glass bottle would return filled to the top, its contents to be sampled by the rest of the family.

Ward and Charlie began whooping and hollering,

and they were soon matched in spirit by their mother, Agnes, and little Sarah. No one else could hear them on this beautiful spring day—their nearest neighbors lived miles away—but that didn't dampen their enthusiasm. Finally, sensing the moment of jubilation was over, Mother directed her daughters back to the cabin to continue their numerous household chores.

As the process continued, Ward readied himself on the rough cottonwood slab that served as a well curb to receive yet another mud-filled bucket. But as he reached for the bucket, the rope suddenly broke, sending the load hurling down toward his unsuspecting father. Ward grasped only handfuls of air as Charlie collapsed on the ground beside him.

Between streaks of mud, Ward's face was white with fear as he peered over the well. Charlie's blue eyes were just visible over the edge of the shaft. Neither boy could speak or breathe. Father must be dead, Charlie thought wildly, not wanting to say anything out loud.

The eerie silence was then shattered by a familiar voice—from below. "What's the matter up there? Have you two fallen asleep?"

Charlie fell back against the mud pile and Ward cleared his throat. "The rope broke, Father."

"Well, send what's left of the rope down and I'll reattach it to the bucket. Then, I'm coming out."

As the seconds turned into minutes, Ward and Charlie couldn't imagine what their father was doing. What they didn't know was that the mud-filled bucket, weighing about sixty pounds, had careened down the well with such force that it had become buried under the earth and had to be dug out. When Father's muddy form surfaced above ground, both boys couldn't wait to hear what had happened.

"It's a funny thing, but I was bent over when the rope broke, so that bucket hit the rim of my hat, and that's all. My hat was buried under the bucket, can you believe that?"

Ward and Charlie stared at him, their mouths open in wonder.

"Is anything wrong, Stewart?" Mother had joined them again after sensing from the cabin window that something was amiss. "Is there water in the well?" she asked anxiously while securing wisps of hair that had escaped her tightly wound bun.

"There's nothing the matter, Sarah, and yes, it looks like we have about five feet of good water." Without another word, Father led the way back to the cabin, the boys and their mother following him single file.

His heart still racing, Charlie wasn't sure his legs would carry him. His father and uncle were both pastors, and he had heard a lot about miracles. Maybe today he had seen one with his own two eyes.

A while later, inside the cabin, Ward began to tell his mother and sisters the whole story. When he had finished, Mother was the first to speak.

"Stewart, I feel like thanking the Father," she said softly.

Wordlessly, every member of the Sheldon family rose from their chairs and got on their knees. Father prayed first and then Mother offered her thanks. With God's help they had survived, and reveled in, another day on the prairie.

Sarah Ward and Stewart Sheldon first met as school-mates in Perry Center, New York, a farming community in the western part of the state. While many years and miles would separate them before their marriage in 1852, they never forgot their early friendship. Both were from Scotch-Irish, Puritan stock; both shared a deep and abiding love of God.

Sarah's pleasant and submissive demeanor, loved and admired by her family, gave no clue that her childhood had been marked by tragedy. Shortly after meeting Stewart, her father, a physician and surgeon, died, and Sarah and her three brothers were sent to live with other relatives. (Sarah's mother could not care for the children, as she suffered from a debilitating heart condition, causing her to be bedridden for much of her life.) The remaining years of Sarah's childhood and adolescence were spent in Cuba, New York. Until her marriage, Sarah Ward never set foot outside of New York State.

In contrast, Stewart, perhaps rebelling against the stability of his youth or simply displaying the sense of wanderlust that was to characterize young Charlie, decided to venture outside New York in his early twenties. Armed with a bachelor's degree from Hamilton College, in 1848 he set off for Labrador, in eastern Canada, and then hopped aboard a boat for a sail around Cape Horn, the southernmost part of South America. After spending a year teaching in a school in Chile, he returned to North America and spent two years working in a mine in California. He finally returned home in 1851, much to the surprise and relief of his distraught family, and began the course of studies that would determine his future: He enrolled at Auburn Theological Seminary, in Auburn, New York. The next year, he and Sarah married, and he became ordained as a Congregational minister in 1854.

Stewart had already served in two small pastorates by the time he and his wife moved to a church in Wellsville, New York, where Charles was born on February 26, 1857. And Wellsville would only be one more stop along the way. From there the young couple and their ever-growing family moved to Central Falls, Rhode Island; Chillicothe, Missouri; LeRoy, New York; and Lansing, Michigan. At Lansing, Stewart, beset with health problems, received some startling news from a local physician. If he wanted to live for two more years—and that was all the doctor gave him—he should move his family west.

But when this nameless medical sage said west, in all likelihood he didn't mean Yankton, Dakota Territory. No one would go to live on the fierce, wide-open prairie for his health. Yet Stewart had a higher calling.

Sarah's brother, Joseph Ward, who years before had lived with the Sheldons while a student at Brown University in Rhode Island, had recently accepted a position as the minister of the First Congregational Church in Yankton. Because First Congregational was the only Congregational church in the entire territory, his task of reaching people throughout the territory became more than humanly possible. After Joseph made a special trip to Lansing—a trip which coincided with the doctor's dire prognosis—Stewart decided to join him. Officially, Stewart would have the title of home missionary superintendent, responsible for church planting in the Dakota Territory. Young Charlie was so excited about the prospect of settling in the West that he convinced Uncle Joe to take him along when he left Lansing. Charlie wanted to be the first of his family to set foot on the prairie.

The Dakota Territory, which encompassed all of present-day North and South Dakota, as well as large portions of Wyoming and Montana and a sliver of Nebraska, had been established on March 2, 1861, by then President James Buchanan. When Abraham Lincoln assumed office, he appointed his personal physician, William Jayne, as the territory's first governor. At the same time, Yankton was recognized as the capital of the Dakota Territory. Although during the 1860s settlement in the territory was sparse, with the arrival of a railroad from Sioux City, Iowa, in 1873, immigrants from Norway, Sweden, Denmark, and

Germany began coming in ever-increasing numbers. Soon the towns of Yankton, Vermillion, and Bon Homme began to show signs of economic prosperity.

The Sheldons arrived around 1867, before this large migration began. In his later years, Charles would describe Yankton as a town made up of cowboys, Indians, saloons, and a red-light district. There was truly a need for men and women of God, and his father's early successes undoubtedly assured the Sheldon family that they were in the right place at the right time. Within ten years Charles's father succeeded in planting almost one hundred churches.

Home for the Sheldons became a homestead claim of 160 acres of tillable farmland. Charles's father had purchased a team of mules, a lumber wagon, and a breaking plow, and with these "tools" he began the arduous task of building his own home. With the help of his sons, he made daily trips to the river, two miles away, where he cut cottonwood trees into logs and hauled them back to the future site of his home.

The finished two-room log cabin became not only the family's refuge from the elements, but their window on history as well. From the front porch they often spied Indians, who lived in tepees at the edge of their property, sitting on the ground a few yards away. They also witnessed George Armstrong Custer and his troops patrolling the area a few years before their controversial actions that led to the Battle of Little Big Horn.

The two rooms of the Sheldon cabin were actually two floors. The upstairs quarters was divided by hanging cloths into bedrooms. But to young Charlie, the downstairs room would be known as the family parlor. That was where the day started, and that was where roots that would not wither, roots of a spiritual nature, were planted.

In the family parlor after breakfast, but before beginning the day's work, family prayers were held. Like everything else in the neatly run Sheldon household, there was a definite order to be followed during these devotions. In the opposite end of the room from where the meal was served, chairs were positioned in a circle, one for each family member. Charlie and Ward tried to sit away from their youngest sisters, but that wasn't always possible. As soon as Father took his chair, the devotions began—and everyone found a seat, regardless of location.

One morning, the family was reading from the Book of Revelation. The reading that day would be a milestone for the family. In his head Charlie calculated that if each person read two verses, why, someone would only have to read one, the last verse of the Bible! As usual, Father began, his ministerial voice conveying a sense of majesty and authority. Mother followed with her two verses, then Ward, as the oldest boy, and Alice, the oldest girl, continued in kind. Charlie cleared his throat and began to read: "And the Spirit and the bride say, Come. And let him that heareth say, Come." From the corner of his eye he could see little Sarah's excitement at the thought of having to read only one verse. Her legs were swinging slightly, though not enough to deserve a reprimand—at least, not yet.

As Sarah was at last handed the family Bible, her little voice wavered. "The grace of our Lord Jesus Christ be with you all. Amen." She then closed the book with an air of triumph, to be stopped short by Father's massive hand on her shoulder.

"That was only one verse, Sarah. Please, begin again at Genesis, book one, verse one," he pronounced firmly.

Charlie couldn't believe they had finally made it through the entire Bible—only to begin again! He couldn't remember when they had started reading the Bible, except that they had never missed a single day. Now they were finished. . .but only for the slightest moment captured by Sarah's elfin grin.

When he heard his mother's soprano, he quickly came back to the present. Sarah had finished her second verse, and the family was now singing a hymn of his mother's choosing. Afterward they would all kneel by their chairs for the morning prayer, offered by Father. Today, after witnessing Sarah's indiscretion and perhaps Charlie's daydreaming, there was no telling how long that prayer might be.

Sure enough, Charlie thought, his eyes peeking through folded fingers, his father had assumed that they were in need of mighty intercession. As Father's voice wavered with emotion, Charlie could just barely see the wheat waiting to be cut, and the barn, where he would start his chores. Minutes later, with Father's final "Amen," the family once again assumed their seats for the last order of business. One by one, each child stood in front of Father and recited the Lord's Prayer out loud and then returned to his or her chair. The tricky part, as Charlie and Ward had discussed often, was in knowing how long to wait after one child had finished before the next could begin. No one questioned their father on any matter, but especially on matters relating to God. Father was adamant that no disrespect be shown, however slight or unintentional. Finally, Father slowly rose from his chair, the signal that the family could begin their various chores.

A team of oxen waited to be harnessed in the barn by Charlie Sheldon.

Charlie wasn't the only child assigned to the hard work of plowing the fields or tending to the animals. All five children were taught to feed the stock, milk the cows, and harness wild horses and stubborn mules. That was only the beginning. There was wood to be chopped, water to be hauled (even after the new well was functioning), and occasional prairie fires to be stopped in their tracks. Then there were the more mundane tasks of sewing and washing clothes and making candles. Lastly, all were responsible for procuring meat for the dinner meal. While they learned to trap coyotes and wolves for their furs, they shot geese, ducks, and chickens for food. Charlie would later write, "If there was anything that Dakota farm taught us all for life, it was the dignity and joy of work with our hands."

When the day's chores were finished, the family shared the kitchen duties with their mother, preparing and cleaning up after the evening meal. That the Sheldons were isolated from civilization was no barrier to amusement. Many evenings were occupied by playing chess, checkers, or backgammon. Charlie, however, pursued a different pastime. After dinner, having made sure that the leaves were removed from the dining room table, he would shove it together to make a small, round table. He then placed a kerosene lamp on top, as well as a plate of cut apples. With his latest book in hand, he settled down for an evening of reading, all the while helping himself to healthy slices of fruit.

Charlie had found a man in Yankton who had an impressive library that contained, among other treasures, the entire set of Sir Walter Scott's *Waverley* novels, as well as numerous volumes of Shakespeare and Dickens. But traveling six miles each way to Yankton occasionally presented unforeseen obstacles.

On horseback one afternoon, Charlie was leaving Yankton, his latest volume of Scott neatly wrapped in a large square of oilcloth, as was his custom. The sky was becoming darker by the minute, and the young boy feared the worst. A terrific thunderstorm, so common to the prairie, was brewing, and there was nothing Charlie could do but ride right through it. The pony was uncharacteristically brave, its pace quickening rather than hesitant, and Charlie knew why. His pony was hungry and would stop at nothing—well, almost nothing—to return to its beloved barn.

As the winds became stronger, however, Charlie wondered if his determination to reach home was pure foolishness. Hail was spitting at his cheeks, his coat was soaked through, and he could see only a few feet in front of him. Patting his chest, he felt the oilcloth-clad novel, which he had buttoned inside his vest for good measure. Several minutes later when the cloudburst had passed, Charlie let out a sigh that he knew was understood by his pony.

Charlie and his pony turned their sights again toward the family homestead, but a quarter of a mile later their journey came to another standstill. A familiar stream in the prairie had turned into a roaring river, increasing with intensity the longer the young traveler waited on its banks. Mulling over his options, Charlie decided to proceed, urging his pony to plunge in against the animal's better instincts. Suddenly, he remembered his book, which soon would be soaked through since the water would be almost over his head. Reaching inside his vest, he pulled the package out and held it over his head. Then, sliding off the pony's back, Charlie grabbed the animal's tail and hung on for dear life, all the while waving the oilcloth bundle in the air. He had seen cowboys make this very same maneuver when crossing rivers on a cattle drive—although not holding a Walter Scott masterpiece. As the pony navigated the raging currents, which occasionally forced them down the stream a bit, Charlie floated behind, eagerly watching the shoreline.

Finally, the exhausted pony struggled to shore and Charlie mounted his slippery back for the ride home. They were safe, and he could only hope that his benefactor's beloved book was not ruined. Once inside the cabin, his fears were laid to rest: The oilcloth, with the assistance of a quick-thinking twelve-year-old boy, had served its purpose.

After a short time on the prairie Charlie had come to know the loving hand of God upon him, upholding his father in the well and the entire family each morning in the parlor. He had witnessed the power of his heavenly Father in the middle of a paralyzing storm, and His grace in again providing a safe journey home. While most days on the homestead were routine, Charlie still felt God's presence in the sheer beauty of his surroundings. The sweep of the prairie, the wide horizon, the exultant pony rides over the prairie flowers and grasses, the seasons of harvest and wheat stacking and threshing and hunting all held an intense fascination for the impressionable adolescent. Now he was about to witness another moment of divine intervention when God would use one of His own in a most powerful way.

Charlie had never liked one particular cow in their

small herd, and he couldn't be persuaded to change his opinion. The Texas cow wasn't much of a milker, was ornery as could be, and wouldn't stay inside the barn-yard fence. It was the last quality that had demanded that Charlie's father use his ingenuity on this balmy summer day. Because all the rest of the Sheldons were in Yankton on errands, Charlie was enlisted to help.

Father had decided to fashion a "poke" or a kind of bonnet around the cow's head so he could lead her to more secure surroundings.

"Just hold her head steady, Charlie," he directed to his wide-eyed son. "She's certainly jumpy, isn't she?"

Charlie could only nod in agreement as the beast struggled and ranted, occasionally plunging her head in wild movements up and down. His eyes were fixed, however, on her long beautiful horns that tapered to points that could gore a man straight through.

"She doesn't look like such a bad cow," Father continued as he tried to find a better way to approach the unruly animal.

"Noooo," answered Charlie slowly. He couldn't help but look into the cow's seemingly gentle brown eyes. All he saw was pure, unadulterated rage.

Finally Father, perspiration running down his face, managed to buckle the poke around the neck of the cow. Saying a silent prayer, Charlie let go of her head and quickly moved to the right. But he was not fast enough or far enough away from the angry beast. In one ferocious gesture, the cow swung her horns and pierced Charlie's right arm just below the biceps muscle. The wound severed an artery and cut straight to the bone, now visible to the terrified boy.

Yelling in pain, Charlie dropped to the ground, holding his arm as blood pulsed wildly through his fingers. The cow was not moved by Charlie's evident distress. She stepped on the writhing boy with all four hooves, wrestled off the poke between the bars of the fence, and then leaped over the railing, galloping with glee across the rolling pasture.

As soon as he was able to assess the situation, Father picked up Charlie in his arms and headed for the cabin. After he had laid the boy down on the floor, Father raced to find any suitable piece of cloth and then fashioned a tourniquet to stop the bleeding.

"Charlie, I've got to go the barn for a tool. You're going to be all right, son," he said in his calmest voice.

Charlie had forced himself to stop crying, but the sight of all his blood on the floor and covering his father's shirt made him feel alternately weak and nauseous. In a minute, his father returned out of breath, a three-cornered harness needle in his hand. He grabbed some white silk thread from the sewing box and threaded it through the needle. Charlie knew his father had never done anything like this before, but the man showed no sign of nervousness. Father's hands were sure and steady as he lifted Charlie's arm and began to sew five stitches across the gaping wound. That finished, Father left on another errand, returning a few minutes later with a bucket of blue mud from their newly dug well.

Squeezing the stones from the mud, Charlie's father packed the blue clay into a ball and slapped it onto the wound. As a final step, he wrapped a towel securely around the boy's arm.

"The mud feels nice and cool," Charlie whispered. "Thank you, Father."

When his mother, brother, and sisters returned from Yankton, they were surprised to find Charlie stretched out in the parlor, and also relieved that Father had known exactly what to do.

"I don't know of anyone else in the Dakota Territory who has a wound sewn up with a harness needle," Mother exclaimed.

"Never mind the territory, Sarah," Father added, a twinkle in his eye. "Maybe in the entire history of surgery!"

Every day Father applied fresh blue mud to Charlie's arm, but only after Mother used hot water to remove the old mud that had hardened from the day before. Unable to perform any chores, Charlie soaked up the attention, enjoying another *Waverley* novel that Alice had managed to borrow for him from his benefactor's library. None of Sir Walter Scott's heroes ever was gored by a Texas cow, he thought to himself from time to time as the weeks went by.

Later that fall the Texas cow was shot near the Missouri River by a neighboring farmer who had tried in vain to catch her. Knowing she was Stewart's cow, the neighbor graciously gave the beef to the Sheldons, a gesture that pleased Charlie in particular.

"The beef sure is tough," Charlie remarked at the dinner table between bites.

"But not as tough as life on the prairie," Mother added.

"And certainly not as difficult as life without our wonderful heavenly Father," Father stated with special emphasis. Someday, Father knew, Charlie would want to make a formal profession of his faith. These "life lessons" on the prairie would not go unheeded.

From their earliest days on the prairie, the Sheldons had attended Uncle Joe's church in Yankton. But because of the distance from the homestead to Yankton, the family attended, for the most part, on Sundays only. That pattern would change during the last winter they lived on the prairie. Uncle Joe began holding revival meetings on weeknights at a small hall in town.

Night after night, Father summoned his children, and Charlie in particular, to the wagon to make the trip into Yankton. Charlie was all too aware of his father's intentions. He knew his father hoped that he would make a public confession of his faith before the meetings ended.

Night after night, Charlie heard the call from Uncle Joe to make a public stand in front of the congregation. But while he wanted to please his father, and while he

27

felt the need to commit his life to Jesus, he somehow lacked the courage to do so.

It was often after midnight before the family returned to their cabin, with just the stars to guide their way. Charlie would retreat wordlessly to his simple bed in the upstairs room. *Lord, please give me the strength to say the words You know I want to say,* he prayed silently. *And if it is Your will, please make it tomorrow night. Amen.*

Charlie knew that to become a Christian was to let others know you were one. With that thought as his guiding force, at last, a few nights later, he decided to make his stand. His knees shaking and his heart wildly beating, Charles Sheldon arose from the wooden bench at Uncle Joe's invitation and joined the others at the front of the hall. When he finally had made the decision and was facing his uncle, he felt a sense of relief sweep over his body and an immense weight depart from his already substantial shoulders.

That night, as the wagon neared the homestead, Father turned to Charlie and said, "Your mother will be so pleased, son. I can't wait to tell her." But as soon as she saw her husband and son, tears began streaming down her face. She threw her arms around Charlie, full of joy over the news that was written across their faces.

Later, Charlie and the others who had gone to the front of the hall had to meet with the church's deacons to answer doctrinal questions that were considered prerequisites to church membership. To the young man who would soon leave home, the questions made little sense. What was important was that his family was proud of him. God had given him the strength to stand up that night.

While most boys living in the Dakota Territory at the time did not attend school, Charlie had not missed a single year, thanks to Uncle Joe. Joseph Ward had become, in addition to pastor, the only teacher in Yankton. Even though classes were held in a cramped law office, Charlie was enthusiastic about going. For one thing, he adored Uncle Joe and wanted to model his life after him.

Joseph Ward, who one day would become president of Yankton College, was an extremely well-educated man for his times. A graduate of the prestigious Phillips Academy in Andover, Massachusetts, as well as of Brown University in Providence, Rhode Island, he instilled in his pupils a love of learning and an abiding sense of decency. He was known for his attention to the less fortunate of his parishioners, a quality Charlie would emulate years later in his own pastorate.

For the first three years Charlie lived in the cabin on the prairie, he attended Uncle Joe's school, sometimes riding his faithful pony—the same one that had weathered the storm out on the prairie—and sometimes walking the six miles to town. The following year, Charlie began attending the Yankton Academy, another of Uncle Joe's inventions. At the same time, to devote himself more to church planting, Father sold the homestead and moved the family into town.

At the academy, Charlie and Ward soon found themselves in a rather awkward, but by no means uncommon, situation. They were the only boys. But it didn't take long for them to get used to being surrounded by so many girls. Besides, they both realized they weren't in a makeshift school anymore. Meant as a stepping-stone to higher learning, the academy stressed, among other subjects, Latin and mathematics. To Charlie, the first was a breeze and the second, an albatross. But two young women in his class were happy to strike a compromise with the handsome but rough-hewn teenager.

"Charlie, I don't understand Livy at all," whined Lily, speaking of a Roman historian whose writings they read in Latin.

"It's almost impossible," echoed her friend Gladys. "Maybe if you could help us, we'd tell you how to use Sturm's theorem to solve the mathematics problems."

Charlie thought for a moment. Obviously everyone realized that he had no head for numbers. "Sounds like a good idea," he quickly agreed.

He wasn't about to question the ethics of such a bargain, not yet at least.

Uncle Joe had plans for Charlie and Ward that he had been discussing with the boys' parents, often late into the night. Uncle Joe wanted Charlie to follow in his footsteps by attending Phillips Academy. Likewise, he wanted Ward to study at Brown University.

One of the requirements for admission to Phillips was a knowledge of Greek, a subject Charlie had not studied. In his final year at the academy, he began immersing himself in Greek paradigms, working alone in one corner of a classroom because no other students were in his situation. While he never felt he came close to becoming a Greek scholar, one of Charlie's great pleasures at the time was studying Homer.

Charlie felt privileged and grateful as he prepared for the day when he would leave Yankton, probably for good. When he finally stepped onto the train that would take him to Chicago and then head toward the East Coast, he imagined a pillar of cloud leading him by day, giving him direction, and a pillar of fire by night, enlightening his thoughts. Years later he described how his mind's eye "went again and again into that end of the log house called the 'parlor,' and saw Father and Mother kneeling there at the family altar. . .every morning at family prayers." It was a picture he would never forget, a poignant reminder of his days on the untamed prairie and the source of all his blessings, in the past and in the days to come.

three

The train ride from Yankton to Chicago and then Chicago to Boston was like a trip back in time. In a few days Charles had gone from a rowdy, albeit sparsely populated, western territory to the birthplace of colonial America. While he had no real memory of his early years in New York State, Charles did feel slightly overwhelmed by the burgeoning metropolises and industrialization that characterized the Northeast. After passing factory upon factory on the way from Boston to Andover, he could not at first distinguish the sturdy industrial brick buildings of Phillips from the rest of the landscape.

Andover itself, in hilly northeastern Massachusetts,

was incorporated in 1646, and owing to its location on the Merrimack and Shawsheen rivers, was indeed a natural industrial site even though it had become better known as a bastion of learning. In a later novel, *The Crucifixion of Philip Strong*, Charles described what was very likely his impression of Andover:

> *The atmosphere of the place is scholastic. You know I passed four years of student life there. With the exception of the schools there are not a thousand people in the village, a quiet, sleepy, dull, retired, studious place. I love the memory of it.*

More recently, Andover had gained fame for being the home of abolitionist Harriet Beecher Stowe, as well as for becoming the center of the antislavery movement. Phillips Andover, a private, religiously oriented boarding school, had been founded in 1778 during the Revolutionary War, hardly an auspicious time for an institution of higher learning to begin. But as the wealthiest colonists began sending their children to Phillips, the academy began to displace the popular Latin grammar schools of the time and to become the school of choice for those most likely to succeed.

Now Charles Monroe Sheldon would join ranks with some of the most affluent young men in America. As the only representative of the Dakota Territory at the school, he would know no one. But he would stand out for other reasons, as well.

Charles was nineteen years old when he began classes at Phillips Andover Academy. He was a strapping young man, having reached his adult height of more than six feet, with well-muscled arms and shoulders, the result of years of hard labor on the homestead. Three years older than most of his classmates, he towered over them physically and emotionally, despite his often harsh self-examination. But he would not overwhelm his peers in the classroom—at least, not yet.

Regrettably, his schooling in Yankton was not sufficient to allow him to enter the academy as a senior. Charles would be forced to enter as a member of the so-called middle class, and thus spend two years instead of one, as he had planned, in Andover.

After a long, lonely walk up a winding hill to the academy buildings, Charles registered for his first term of classes in a little office, surrounded by homesick boys. At the same time, he received his room assignment and met the boy who would be his roommate. Almost as tall as Charles, a pleasant surprise, his handshake was weak and lifeless.

"Charles Sheldon," the older boy announced.

"Henry Alford," the other intoned.

To Charles, they seemed like two strange dogs meeting each other in a new neighborhood. *If we ever have to settle our differences with our fists,* Charles mused, *I'll surely have the upper hand.*

Charles and Henry agreed who would have which

bedroom and then wordlessly began to unpack their belongings. Charles, who had traveled light, finished quickly and then began assessing his new quarters. There were two bedrooms and one study room, as well as one window at the end of the room that overlooked the campus. In the months to come, Charles would discover a use for the window besides ventilation. It would become a handy depository for all the ashes that accumulated in the little stove that heated their room. If these deposits took place when a group of boys was below, so much the better!

The stove, coincidentally, would become a source of contention between the two roommates as the seasons began to change and a legendary New England winter gripped the campus. Charles and Henry had agreed early on to a division of duties: Charles would sweep out the rooms, get the water each day for their wash basins, and bring up the coal, and Henry would build the fires, as well as sweep down the stairs when necessary. "But only down one flight to the next landing," Henry quickly added.

Predictably during one of the most frigid weeks, trouble set in. Late one night the fire went out, and in the morning the roommates awoke shivering—and angry. "Well, go on, make the fire, Henry," Charles directed.

"If you had performed your duties, perhaps I'd be more willing to do mine," Henry countered rather mysteriously.

"What do you mean by that?"

"Just what I said. I don't believe that you've been bringing me my proper amount of water." Henry sat on his bed, wrapped in blankets, his lips almost turning blue. Even so, he would not budge.

So the stalemate began, one that would last a week. Neither Charles nor Henry would build a fire. Both young men sat huddled in their overcoats, often overlaid with blankets to survive the bitter cold. This continued until their situation came to the attention of the principal, Dr. C. F. P. Bancroft, known lovingly as "Banty" to the boys.

After hearing both sides of their dilemma, Dr. Bancroft ordered Henry to build the fire, a command that caused Charles to beam with pleasure. He was about to break into a chuckle when he was stopped, mouth agape, by the next words of the principal.

"Sheldon, I didn't think you were such a fool, even if you did have the right of it," he advised rather sternly and turned to go.

At that Charles and Henry looked at each other rather sheepishly and then laughed and shook hands, their hostilities gone. Charles would remember Banty's parting words for a long time. Indeed, why should he suffer, or allow someone else to suffer, when he had the power to end his distress with a simple gesture? Perhaps he wasn't as mature as he thought. Perhaps he needed these two years to grow.

An integral part of Charles's education at Phillips had

nothing to do with book learning. Because his parents could pay only part of his expenses at the academy, Charles was forced to hold several part-time jobs over the course of two years.

During the first winter he swept the floors of the academy building where he had registered for his first classes. Wednesday and Saturday afternoons would find the earnest young man hard at work—for the most part. Saturdays were the hardest because that was when he could hear the cheering at baseball or football games on the playing fields nearby. Occasionally he would stop and crane his neck out the window, wishing he could be cheering on the home team, too.

Charles earned three dollars a week sweeping floors, more than enough to cover the weekly room and board fee of $1.75.

The following year he was hired to replace the broken windows in the building known as the Commons. Every winter, several panes would be knocked out, the result of errant snowballs. In addition, Charles was responsible for pumping the bellows of the organ during the mandatory Sunday chapel services (held both morning and afternoon), as well as for serving as something of a personal assistant for a professor at Andover Theological Seminary. Once he fell asleep during the chapel service—Sundays were when he caught up with his sleep in those days—and suffered the embarrassment of the hymn beginning with no organ music.

But it was his position as professorial assistant that would prove to be the most unusual. Every night during the winter of his senior year, Charles reported to the home of Professor Austin Phelps at a few minutes before seven o'clock. After being let in by one of the professor's elderly servants, Charles would make his way upstairs to the distinguished gentleman's bedroom. For the next hour, Charles proceeded to give Professor Phelps a foot massage. The young man had been given exact instructions on the proper massage technique, and within a week he seemed to have mastered the movements.

At precisely eight o'clock, the massage ended and Charles proceeded on to his next task: reading out loud. Naturally, the nightly selections were chosen ahead of time by the professor himself, and all were selected with the purpose of putting him to sleep. The professor suffered from terrible insomnia, as well as hypochondria, and could think of no better sleep inducer than listening to a lengthy tome.

At precisely nine o'clock, with the professor comfortably dozing, Charles made his way downstairs, where he would occasionally be offered cold milk and a sandwich. Sometimes he would be asked to write a letter for the professor's daughter, Elizabeth Stuart Phelps, herself a distinguished author. This pleased Charles greatly as he himself had thoughts of pursuing a writing career, a dream he had, in fact, started to make a reality back in Yankton.

Influenced by Sir Walter Scott and his *Waverley* novels, Charles began composing stories at night in the log cabin. When a few of his stories were accepted for publication by the Yankton newspaper (for no fee), Charles began to dream bigger dreams. After sending numerous efforts to well-known periodicals and newspapers around the country, he finally sold an article to a small newspaper in Boston. But there had been far more rejections than acceptance letters, the story of most aspiring writers. Still, his dream remained alive just by being in the presence of Elizabeth Phelps.

As all writers thrive on great writing, Charles saved whatever money he could to purchase books just for himself. Often there wasn't much money left over after paying for board and fuel and clothing, and the erstwhile Dickens was left with a critical decision.

During the Thanksgiving holiday, Henry had left for the weekend to visit his family in New Hampshire, leaving Charles little to do except, of course, build the fire in the stove. Rousing himself from his lethargy, Charles suddenly stood and clapped his hands. "Why, I'll go to Boston by myself!" he cried out in his empty room.

Charles had been to Boston a few times before, and on one of those trips he had discovered a wonderful old bookstall called the Archway. There were new and secondhand books at the Archway, and Charles had become something of a bargain hunter as he perused the stacks. On this particular trip, Charles, feeling the weight of coins in his pocket, fully intended to spend time at the Washington Street bookstall.

Running his fingers down the spines of leather-bound volumes, Charles almost shouted when he came across a title he very much wanted to read. It was Victor Hugo's *Les Miserables,* translated by Cournal, a red-bound book printed on good quality paper. The price, he discovered upon inquiring, was exactly one dollar. Without thinking, Charles bought the book and left the stall, satisfied beyond description. Then the reality of his situation caused him to stop in his tracks.

The train ride home cost sixty-three cents. Charles had seventeen cents left in his pocket.

He had no choice but to walk back to Andover, a distance of twenty-odd miles, and he would have to accomplish the feat in less than ideal conditions. A crust of snow lay on the ground, and it was just starting to drizzle. After spending his last coins on a cup of coffee and a sandwich, he began his journey, arriving in his room sometime after two in the morning. While his overcoat was soaked through, his prize purchase had remained dry, tucked inside his shirt.

As the dawn peeked through the curtains, Charles slowly closed the book, turned out his German student lamp—he had finished Book One—and went to sleep. He had survived another adventure unscathed, something that could not be said for Hugo's famed protagonist Jean Valjean! It was worth every soggy mile to go to bed with Hugo's beautiful prose running through his head.

Charles had followed in Uncle Joe's steps by attending Phillips, and now he would continue on the path trod by his beloved mentor by going on to Brown University in Providence, Rhode Island. From the sixty students, including Charles, who graduated from Phillips Academy in 1879, six joined him at Brown. Most of the rest made plans to attend Yale, Amherst, Harvard, or Princeton.

But Uncle Joe wasn't the only reason Charles had made up his mind to attend Brown. His best friend from his two years at Phillips was going there, too. For the next four years M. C. Gile would be Charles's roommate; for the rest of their lives, they would remain friends. Charles was likely remembering his friendship with Gile years later in writing *The Crucifixion of Philip Strong* when he stated, "The love of men for men in the strong friendship of school and college life is one of the marks of human divinity."

After such a fine start at Phillips, college presented few problems academically for Charles. He breezed through geometry, trigonometry, and calculus—achievements he would have enjoyed sharing with the young women of the Yankton Academy—but algebra problems remained a stumbling block. Despite the efforts of several teachers, as well as his roommate M. C., Charles could not master the subject. In the humanities, he seemed to find his niche in classical languages, and his writing also improved.

So interested was he in writing that Charles decided to join the literary fraternity Delta Upsilon, a group of men who met every Friday night to discuss and critique their latest work. From these associations came the opportunity to submit more articles for publication, and at the time the publication of choice for aspiring Brown University writers was a magazine called *Youth's Companion*. During his four years at Brown, Charles submitted hundreds of articles—and had about a dozen of them actually published. He would write, years later, of the joy he felt upon receiving "the first yellow slip of a check" from *Youth's Companion,* a check made out to him for the incredible amount of two dollars. Sometimes, for a longer article, he would even receive five dollars!

As always, money remained an overriding concern for him. One winter he and a friend taught in a night school in Providence that was geared to working men and boys. In his words, there was a good deal more "lickin' " than "larnin' " going on at the school. One summer he worked as a waiter at the Pavilion Hotel in Wolfeboro, New Hampshire, on Lake Winnepesaukee, and between his junior and senior years he worked "slinging clams" at a resort on Narragansett Bay in Rhode Island. His tenure as a waiter was distinguished by an oversized tip given by a patron who heard Charles quote from Homer (the patron was a classical

Greek scholar). His time spent as a clam slinger was only distinguished by his appetite for fresh and delicious seafood.

Still, despite these secular pursuits, Charles came to a major life decision at the conclusion of his junior year. He would become a minister and would continue his education at Andover Theological Seminary upon graduation from Brown. His decision wasn't all that surprising, considering his admiration for his uncle and father, and it wasn't all that remarkable considering his church involvement in Providence. He had joined the Round Top Congregational Church as a freshman and quickly volunteered his services both as a member of the bass section in the choir and as a Sunday school teacher.

But his role in the church would soon change dramatically, thanks to Lee Wong. Every week as Charles deposited his soiled clothes at Lee Wong's Chinese laundry, the college student tried to think of something to say to the pleasant man. Mr. Wong spoke little English but was obviously eager to learn and eager to make friends.

"You go to church?" Mr. Wong questioned one day as he sorted Charles's shirts.

Charles seemed to perk up at the question. He had been coming here week after week and had never inquired about Mr. Wong's faith!

"Would you like to come with me?" he said slowly.

Smiling, Mr. Wong nodded his head excitedly. "Oh,

yes. My friends come, too?"

As Charles was to discover the following Sunday, Mr. Wong meant his fifteen Chinese friends, the entire population of Chinese laundrymen living in Providence. For a while, Charles escorted the group every Sunday to the worship service at Round Top, even though he knew they could understand little of the pastor's sermon. Then Charles had a better idea.

"Mr. Wong, how would you and your friends like to have your very own Sunday school class? You could learn about Jesus, and you could learn English, too."

Smiling as always, Lee Wong nodded, not sure what he had agreed to. Starting the following Sunday at four o'clock in the afternoon, as Charles liked to say, "the first Sunday school for Chinese laundrymen" began. With the Bible as their "English textbook," Mr. Wong and his friends learned English and received a little Christian education, too. After three years in Sunday school, they were all considered fluent in their adopted language.

Charles had recognized a need in his community, reached out in friendship to those who needed help, and organized a response based in the church. He was still following in Uncle Joe's steps and in his father's, but he was also treading closely behind One whom he had just begun to know.

Just down the road from Phillips Academy, Andover Theological Seminary seemed an obvious choice for

Charles. The seminary had been founded early in the nineteenth century by the Congregational church but had a tradition of much more conservative leanings than many Congregational seminaries of the day. Instead of embracing a more Unitarian philosophy as Harvard's seminary had, Andover chose to blend Calvinist teachings with its Congregationalist theology.

Charles would enter Andover as a member of the class of 1886, having graduated from Brown University in 1883. Little did he realize that the seminary he was entering was no longer a bastion of conservatism, and during his school years, Andover would become a veritable hotbed of controversy.

The controversy at Andover began, simply enough, with the retirement of Professor E. A. Park in 1881. As the voices expounding more liberal theology at the seminary cried out to be heard, the seminary began publishing its own theological journal, the *Andover Review*, in 1884. The purpose of the journal was clearly stated: to rethink and restate Christian theology in contemporary terms. Among the doctrines explored under the heading "Progressive Orthodoxy" was the concept that became known as "future probation" or "second probation."

Future probation, or the teaching that those who did not have the opportunity to accept or reject the Gospel of Jesus Christ during their lifetimes will get another chance in the afterlife and then be judged, was first introduced in America by Newman Smyth, the brother of Andover seminary's president, Egbert C. Smyth. The doctrine went on to state that if God did not make Himself known to a person during that person's lifetime, He would do so in a future state.

But what came to be known as the Andover Controversy went far beyond the issue of future probation. Salvation by the development of moral character became the popular philosophy, fueled by Charles Darwin's theory of evolution. This radical interpretation of salvation, it was believed by Andover's faculty, was necessary to attempt to address the social problems of the day.

During Charles's years at Andover, fierce debate arose over the issue of future probation, a debate that would divide pastors all over New England and cause E. C. Smyth, among others at the seminary, to face charges of treason and heresy. (After Smyth was dismissed from the seminary in 1887, he appealed his case to the Massachusetts Supreme Court and the decision was reversed. The matter was dropped following a new trial a few years later.) Charles himself, though, perhaps in an effort to distance him from the cauldron of controversy, began advocating what he called "untheological Christianity."

Remembering the success of his efforts with Lee Wong and the way Uncle Joe reached out to the poorest settlers in Yankton, Charles began advocating Christian action instead of a lot of theorizing which, to him, was a waste of time. There was plenty that the world needed; there was plenty that he could do in the spirit of Christian love.

Charles followed a basic course of study at Andover, taking classes in Hebrew, New Testament Greek, church history, homiletics, and elocution. Concerning "sermon making," as he liked to call it, Charles felt his education left something to be desired. He felt totally inadequate to "preach to boys and girls or meet the needs of common men and women." When he was first allowed to preach as a pulpit supply preacher during his senior year, he felt as if he had been thrown into deep water without a life preserver. It would be years before he would adopt his seemingly effortless sermon style, one in which he became famous for using no notes at all.

Besides the fees received from pulpit supply, Charles was also pocketing some change from his writing, which seemed to flourish during his years at Andover. He continued submitting articles to *Youth's Companion,* and many found their way to publication. The industrious young man met the annual expenses of attending seminary—what was at the time the large sum of four hundred dollars a year—with little difficulty. But by his senior year, the question of permanent employment was understandably at the forefront of his mind. And his class faced an unusual situation.

The controversy of future probation, which had made such an impression on Charles's years at Andover, was attached to all the seminary students. It was assumed by churches that anyone who attended

Andover held to the teaching of future probation, and no church wanted a new preacher who had lived and breathed that doctrine. Like all members of his graduating class, Charles was regarded with suspicion "as tainted with dangerous heresy."

Finally, he received a job offer, but it was not exactly what he was looking for. Lyman Abbott, the editor of *The Outlook,* an independent New York religion journal, had apparently noticed Charles's name in print, thanks to *Youth's Companion,* and wanted him to join his editorial staff. Abbott was, in fact, offering Charles the chance to start his own department, an amazing offer for a young man just out of college, and Charles was sorely tempted.

To think things over, Charles retreated to Salem, Massachusetts, where his parents had recently moved. "I've been trained to be a minister, not a journalist," he began one evening over the dinner table.

"Let's start praying right now, son," Stewart Sheldon responded. "God will use you when and how He wishes. He may be preparing your heart as we speak." His wise eyes bore into Charles's, cutting to his core. Together with Charles's mother, they held hands and bowed their heads. Immediately the seminary graduate was transported back to the log cabin and the family parlor, to those mornings, now treasured, when the family united in prayer.

But there was no barn outside, no plowing to be done, no wheat fields waiting to be harvested. Or were there?

four

Waterbury, Vermont, 1886

Charles Sheldon's years of seminary training, however suspect they might have seemed to many churches, were not about to go to waste. Shortly after Lyman Abbott offered him a job at the magazine, Charles received his first pastoral call from the Congregational church in Waterbury, Vermont. He was not needed until October, however, and that was months away.

Charles was twenty-nine years old, and he had been in school for nine straight years. When he wasn't studying, he was working to make ends meet. With the same sense of wanderlust that had once propelled his father to travel to the southernmost point of South

America, Charles hungered to go to England. But he hadn't one cent to his name.

One evening he presented his dilemma to his parents, with whom he was living.

"How much do you think you'll need, Charlie?" his father asked, sincerely concerned. In truth, he didn't see how he could help him, but it didn't hurt to listen.

"I think I could make it to England and back on two hundred dollars, Father," Charles said confidently.

His mother quickly clamped her hand over her mouth to stifle a gasp. Better not to say anything than to belittle his dream, she thought and returned to her needlework.

The sum that Charles had quoted stayed in his father's mind during the next week. When asked by a close friend how Charles was doing, Stewart, deciding he had nothing to lose and knowing his friend to be as thrifty as he, revealed his son's latest quandary. Little did he realize how providential that conversation was to be.

A few days later, an envelope arrived at the Sheldon household, addressed to Charles Sheldon. Inside were crisp bills, with a note attached:

Dear Charles,

After hearing of your desire to go to England, I decided to do everything I could to send you on your way. This is a loan, but one without interest, and one you should pay back

*only after you have begun receiving a salary.
Bon voyage!*

With one small bag, Charles set sail on the Cunard steamer *Cephalonia* from Boston to Liverpool, England. His passage across the Atlantic would cost thirty-five dollars, leaving him with only about $160 for the rest of his trip. But that was just enough for the resourceful young seminary graduate to live on for the next two months, months spent listening to the greatest preachers in Europe, strolling through Westminster Abbey, and occasionally selling stories to popular magazines to get by in a pinch. When he returned to the United States at the beginning of September 1886, Charles had just fifteen cents and an English farthing in his pocket. He succeeded in pawning one of his few assets, his watch, and thus was able to take the train from New York home to Salem, Massachusetts.

His father would need to pay Charles's way to Waterbury, Vermont. Charles Sheldon would arrive in the quiet hill town with empty pockets but an ambitious spirit and a genuine desire to love his new church and honor his first ministry.

There were only two churches in Waterbury, Methodist and Congregational. As in most New England towns, the Congregational church was called the Congo church, and the people were largely conservative. Located in north central Vermont, the picturesque town of seven hundred was planted among the Green Mountains and along the banks of the Winooski Stream.

In his 1893 novel *Robert Hardy's Last Days,* Charles would draw on his fond recollections of Vermont: "Yet, as he looked, somehow there stole into his thought the memory of the old New England home back in the Vermont hills, and the vision of that quiet little country village. . . . He seemed to see the old meeting-house on the hill, at the end of a long, elm-shaded street that straggled through the village. . . ."

The Congregational church of Waterbury was organized according to traditional New England dictates. Two groups made up the congregation: church members and the parish, a group of attendees who did not belong to the church. Both groups could vote on a pastor, and in Charles's case, both had voted him in. Pews in the church were literally owned by the heads of families and could be included as bequests in wills. In Waterbury there was a proper way of doing things that befitted a man of God, and Charles was determined to be that man.

He was offered the yearly salary of eight hundred dollars, but without room and board. To meet that need, he obtained a room, with meals included, at a hotel on the main street of town. It cost four dollars a week. In a few months, living as frugally as he could, he managed to pay back the loan to his father's friend that had financed his sojourn abroad.

For a while, Charles's days were consumed with

visiting the people of his church. As most of his congregation lived outside of town, that meant long rides in a rickety buggy guided by an old pony that had been given him by the retiring minister. The pony, named Pony Bly, was a favorite of children around town, and Charles soon found out why. The beloved minister had always insisted boys and girls and even young men and women ride with him whenever he made his rounds.

Even though he was twenty-nine years old, Charles was still shy around members of the opposite sex. He didn't feel comfortable riding with young women, and he certainly didn't want to be seen with little girls, either. To offend no one (he hoped), he decided at the outset he would make only solitary trips with Pony Bly.

His nights were no different. To maintain his pristine image, he spent every evening, often until midnight or one in the morning, ensconced in his little corner room of the hotel, writing out, word for word, his Sunday sermons. Privately, he wondered when he would feel comfortable preaching, when it would seem like he was talking to his audience as if in conversation instead of delivering a lecture. As he labored, he often would have his meals in his room. His understanding landlady, a woman he came to call affectionately "Mother Barrett," gave him unlimited access to the hotel's pantry. After a couple of generous slices of apple pie, topped with cheese, and two tall glasses of cold milk, Charles would feel fortified and inspired.

Even though he appeared insulated from the rest of the world, Charles had his eyes wide open. There was work to be done, and the town of Waterbury would never be the same.

The Congregational church of Waterbury was flanked by two private homes: one belonging to the former governor of Vermont and occupied by several unmarried lawyers, and the other the residence of an elderly woman, Mrs. Merriam.

Mrs. Merriam, a lifelong resident of Waterbury, had her own pew very near the front of the church where she sat ramrod straight every Sunday, her head tilted just slightly to catch Charles's every word. Unlike some of the other matrons, she seemed very friendly toward Charles and always gave his hand a gentle squeeze as she departed from the church. "Don't forget, I live right next door, Reverend Sheldon," she admonished with a smile. "Perhaps Monday morning you might find time—?"

Charles had wanted to cultivate her friendship, and she had just given him the opportunity on a silver platter. "Of course, Mrs. Merriam. Say, around ten o'clock?"

Mondays at Mrs. Merriam's soon became a standing appointment for the young pastor. In the petite elderly woman, Charles found a sympathetic ear—as well as a very discreet one. He soon felt free to discuss the affairs of the church with her and to gauge the effectiveness of his proposals by her responses.

"Mrs. Merriam, I've been thinking quite a bit about

the young people of Waterbury," he began one Monday.

"Yes, Reverend Sheldon," Mrs. Merriam typically answered.

"They have nowhere uplifting to go at night and on the weekends, nowhere where their minds can be stimulated."

"What exactly are you proposing, if I may ask?" his ever-interested listener queried.

"Well, I haven't thought of a formal proposal, but I am considering starting a reading club for them. Something for them to do besides dancing and card playing!"

At that, Mrs. Merriam stopped rocking in her chair, dropped her crochet work in her lap, and nodded her head vigorously. "Yes, yes, you are right. Dancing and card playing are not healthy pursuits. But where would they meet?"

"Why, at the church, I thought. Do you think they would come—I mean, to discuss a great work of literature?"

That day Charles left Mrs. Merriam's eager to follow his idea as far as he could. After securing the permission from both church members and parish attendees, he wrote out announcements and distributed them. He spread the message during his pastoral visits. Because many of the young people in Waterbury attended the Methodist church, Charles did not want to antagonize their pastor by appearing to try to win them over to his congregation.

But win them over he soon did, much to his surprise. The first winter of Charles's stay in Waterbury, almost one hundred young men and women gathered at the Congo church, eager for social interaction and, of course, the opportunity to discuss *A Tale of Two Cities*. Many of them had come over from the Methodist church, and many came back for Sunday services, too. Charles's fresh approach was appealing and they were interested in what else he had to say. Besides, he was not that much older than they, but he had seen a bit more of the world.

The success of the reading club had created another need in the mind of the enthusiastic new pastor. Waterbury had no town library, and Charles soon set to work to secure the funds to start one. During the campaign, Mrs. Merriam, as usual, was his biggest supporter, enlisting her friends to contribute to his worthy cause. In later years Charles would admit that the library was one of his proudest achievements.

Although Charles continued to depend on Mrs. Merriam, his newfound confidence had launched him into a radical new outreach. He needed to get better acquainted with everyone in his congregation, and what better way than to practically live with them? Thus was born Charles's idea of "boarding around," a plan that began a few months after his arrival. Surprisingly to Charles, the plan was openly accepted, even though the congregation had a reputation for being firmly established in tradition and what had always been done.

Beginning on Sundays, right after church, Charles would join one family for their noontime meal and a few hours of conversation. He would return home to his hotel to spend the night and then come back to the same family's home on Monday, and every day until Saturday, to join them for lunch and dinner (he would have breakfast at his hotel). Charles assumed that conversation would most naturally flow over meals and that folks would be most relaxed. He simply wanted to get to know the family. During the first year of his pastorate, Charles managed to board around with forty families, playing with their children, taking long walks with beleaguered farmers, and sometimes introducing family worship into the homes. (Meanwhile, Mother Barrett reserved slices of apple pie for him whenever he returned to the hotel for the evening.)

Besides wanting to learn the spiritual concerns of the families, Charles also was interested in their concerns for the community. He was becoming known in Waterbury for his "untheological" approach to Christianity, demonstrated by his bringing the young people to church for a reading club. During the week he spent at the home of the president of the Ladies' Aid Society, Charles was alerted to another problem, one that caused great distress for many housewives.

Main Street in Waterbury was like most great thoroughfares of small-town America in 1890: It was unpaved, and it was dusty. During dry seasons, wagons rolling into town would stir up great clouds of dust that would then billow through open windows, causing spotless parlors to become pigpens—or so Waterbury's fastidious housekeepers thought. And to the Ladies' Aid Society president, the presence of dust was not just a sign of slovenliness. Dust was a sin.

This was a problem tailor-made for an inventive young pastor like Charles Sheldon. He had received little education in the natural sciences, but he possessed a mechanical mind, a talent inherited from his resourceful father. An idea in mind, Charles recalled a spring in a hillside just outside of Waterbury that might work perfectly. He mentioned it one Monday to Mrs. Merriam.

"I know exactly where you mean, Reverend Sheldon," the white-haired woman responded, her knitting needles clicking furiously. "That just so happens to be on the property of Angus McDermott, a church member," she continued, with special emphasis on the word member.

Charles looked at her knowingly, their eyes meeting for a brief moment. Angus would be especially helpful if he knew the entire town would know about it—and if the pastor of his church made a special plea to him.

Sure enough, Angus was more than happy to let his spring be part of a town experiment. "But Pastor, the spring is too far from Main Street. You'd have to be making many trips and who'd want to do that?" he queried as he and Charles surveyed the water supply.

Charles had a plan. If he could connect a pipe from the spring to Main Street. . .but he would need a trough or tub large enough to store the water there until it was needed. Again with Mrs. Merriam's help, he found an old barn off the main thoroughfare that had a discarded tub from an old cider press just sitting in the hayloft. Now the water could flow from the spring through the pipe and into the tub!

His next task was to find a "water wagon," a vehicle that could be used to sprinkle water on the dusty road. He found another old cider tub and mounted it onto the back of a lumber wagon. With the help of a local tinsmith, a tin sprinkler was fashioned that would be fastened to the bottom of the tub.

Next Charles had to enlist the help of a driver, and he found such a man in the person of Angus's older brother, Willy. Willy, who looked more like a scarecrow than a man, was something of a town character, but he owned a team of horses—one qualification— and he was more than willing to help Pastor Sheldon.

Finally, the day came when the water wagon would take its maiden voyage down Main Street. Almost everyone from Waterbury and the outlying farms had come to town, and the street was lined with people on both sides. Gazing down from the balcony outside his hotel room, Charles couldn't help but think that more folks had turned out for this than came to both churches in Waterbury on any Sunday!

He took a deep breath as he watched Willy direct

the wagon to the barn where the tub would be filled with water. That done, the older man grabbed the reins and motioned his team to move to the head of the street, careful not to collide with the trees as the wagon turned around. The moment had come, and Willy was all smiles as he drove slowly, the sprinkler spraying water on the dusty road below. As the crowd cheered him on, Willy rode back and forth until the entire street was sufficiently saturated.

"Pastor Sheldon, it's better than the circus!" shouted one boy to Charles, and Charles had to agree.

Throughout that summer and the next, Willy was summoned to perform his amazing feat, much to the delight of the president of the Ladies' Aid Society and all the women who kept house along Main Street. While Charles did have to repair the pipe from time to time, the benefits far outweighed the occasional inconvenience. For the remainder of his ministry at Waterbury, the women in the Ladies' Aid Society would be among his most vocal supporters.

Charles began to notice a curious thing during his first winter in Waterbury. At first, he dismissed the strange occurrence as a natural part of life in small-town, rural America. Young men were dying at an alarming rate, or so he thought, and as their pastor, Charles was being called on to perform funeral after funeral.

While he puzzled over the cause of these deaths, he was forced to confront the rigors of a proper funeral service and burial. First, the families expected a long, belabored sermon in the church, which called to mind every nuance of the departed. Then came the slow buggy ride to the cemetery, which was nine miles outside of town, followed by another almost endless eulogy at the grave. In the winter, with temperatures falling several degrees below zero, Charles found this rite almost impossible to bear since all men were required to remove their hats.

He found little sympathy from Mrs. Merriam. She fully expected to be accorded the same respect when her time came. "The senior deacons have complained, Pastor Sheldon," she said, pouring tea one morning. "They won't stand for you wearing your hat by the grave, and I can't say I blame them."

Charles groaned inwardly at her words. It had only happened once, at a service for a boy whose family hadn't attended church in years. But still his action had made an impression. Like the family-owned pews, this was one thing Charles was not going to be able to change.

"They do approve of the new hearse, though. It's comforting to know that when my time comes, I'll arrive at the cemetery in style," she said, chuckling softly.

Charles nodded, smiling, not willing to discuss the imminence of his dear friend's demise. The new hearse was the result of an accident during one funeral procession. Suddenly the box containing the casket had careened out of the wagon in front of him, landing at the hooves of a trembling Pony Bly! The next Sunday Charles began literally passing the hat for funds to purchase an official hearse. It would be used more than he thought in the months and years ahead.

Of special concern to Charles as the winter began to wain was the cause of all these deaths. Between November 1886 and April 1887, twenty-five young men perished because of a strange illness marked by a high fever. They had all lived on farms outside Waterbury. To pursue the matter, Charles decided to enlist the help of a young physician in town.

Over the next two years, Charles and the doctor were able to pinpoint the cause of death. On the farms where these young men lived, the drinking water came from wells that were located extremely close to the pigpens. It was obvious to the doctor that the water had become contaminated, causing the boys to come down with what looked like typhoid fever.

Charles needed to tell these farm families the truth before more deaths occurred. From his boarding-around visits, he knew his task wouldn't be easy. These rural New Englanders wanted only to believe that providence had claimed their sons' lives. Still, they needed to be told, and to bolster his courage, Charles took the young doctor with him.

At the first farm, he and the doctor were driven off the premises. The farmer even watched Charles's buggy until it disappeared over a hill, just to make sure he wouldn't come back. Although that wouldn't happen again, the reception they received from other families was icy and reserved. Unfortunately, the second winter of Charles's pastorate, he had just as many funerals as during his first few months—and most of them were held for young Vermont farm boys. Shortly afterward, though, some of Charles's ideas were implemented, and pigpens were relocated. Progress could be maddeningly slow in Waterbury.

Still, by all accounts, Charles had accomplished much during his first year in Waterbury. Most folks knew him as the fellow who sprinkled Main Street, or the young man with newfangled notions who told farmers to move their pigpens, or the buttoned-down preacher who frowned on card playing and dancing. Indeed, Charles viewed his activities in the community as an outreach of his pulpit.

But he didn't want to be remembered solely for how he served Waterbury. He wanted to make a difference in the lives of those entrusted to him, his church members and parishioners.

At first, Charles's innovations inside the Congo church were simply interesting. Churchgoers were surprised one Sunday early in 1888 to see a blackboard on top of an easel near the pulpit. As they filed into their pews, Charles picked up the chalk and began to print with large, legible letters. He was writing the Scripture verses for the day, as well as an outline of his sermon.

"This way, you can follow along with me," he explained. "You'll also know when I'm almost done," he added with a twinkle in his eye.

In the Sundays that followed, Charles noticed his elderly members looking not at him but at the blackboard. Sometimes older couples would turn to each other, whispering furiously and shaking their heads. He knew many were losing their hearing, but he had no idea how little they could actually hear. His voice simply was not loud enough to reach them.

Thus was born his next idea, one that started on a small scale. Once a month Charles printed his sermon for the following Sunday and distributed it as people entered the church. The response was overwhelming, according to Mrs. Merriam, who considered herself an accurate gauge of the town's sentiments.

"Not many can hear so well, Reverend Sheldon. They certainly don't have my sharp faculties, as I'm sure you've noticed!" she proclaimed one Monday.

"But do you think once a month is enough?" Charles asked.

"Every Sunday would be best, if you can tolerate the rustling of papers," she said, and then smiled. "Of course, that will only bother those under the age of fifty!"

After working out an arrangement with the operator of the local printing press, Charles took her advice. Each Sunday, that day's sermon was distributed to everyone attending the morning worship service. But they weren't the only ones who wanted to know what the young preacher was saying. Soon half of Waterbury wanted copies of Charles's sermons. In a few months Charles had gone from printing seventy-five copies to more than three hundred, distributing them at the local post office and in stores, as well as in the sanctuary. At the same time, he also began printing outlines of the following week's sermon so listeners would know where he was leading them. He encouraged them to write out their questions and ask him after the morning worship or during the evening service.

Charles's sermons had become more interesting, too. He would often bring a flower, stone, or other visual aid to illustrate his talks. Folks would look up from their handout to the pulpit and back down at their papers to get the full effect of what he was saying.

Soon Charles had another idea. The Congregational church occupied a sizable lot in the center of Waterbury that was used for nothing except to grow grass. After obtaining the deacons' permission, Charles decided to make good use of the land, again as an outreach. Mornings when he wasn't visiting he could be found, spade in hand (one that he had borrowed), digging up his new garden. He purchased seed from his own salary. As spring turned to summer in 1888, so Charles's lovingly tended seeds poked through the rich earth. He had planted a variety of vegetables, and soon the fruits of his labors were evident.

It wasn't long before Mother Barrett from the hotel

came by, asking if she could buy some vegetables for her kitchen. Charles gladly complied. Pretty soon word got out to the rest of town, and Charles was filling as many orders as he could handle. He gave all the money he earned to the church to be used to help the needy and to support foreign missions.

Charles loved to talk to whoever stopped by his garden while he was working. Occasionally he would stand, wipe his forehead with his handkerchief, and gaze out at Main Street, not far away. He knew everyone in Waterbury by now, and he had a friendly wave for all. When the stagecoach dropped off passengers, he liked to see who was back in town or who was leaving for a spell.

Months later, he would wonder. Did he see her and not realize who she was?

five

Mary Abby Merriam—known to all as May—had made this trip a few times before, but this would be her last. As the stagecoach made its way up and down the hilly terrain and around curving roads, the young woman looked out the scratched window and sighed. How she loved Vermont: the towering pines, outrageous wildflowers, and the rolling hills! All too soon she would be leaving this beloved countryside for Kansas, a name that, to her, held no allure.

Her father had been ill for some time, and his condition had puzzled the local physician. Shaking her dark curls, she remembered the pat solution offered by the doctor. "I suggest you move to a healthier climate,

Everet," he pronounced with authority. "Out West would be best. . .perhaps Kansas, the new land of opportunity!"

And so the decision had been made for her and her mother. In a few months they would leave for Topeka, Kansas, never to return to Vermont. This would be her farewell visit to Waterbury, and to her grandmother.

It took the coach three hours to cover a distance of eighteen miles, so winding and tortuous were the country roads. Finally alighting on the dusty street, the young woman broke into a brilliant smile. She had such good memories of this charming New England village, the well-kept white wooden homes, the delightful elderly minister and his dependable pony. What was that creature's name, she asked herself as she collected her suitcases and made her way down the familiar street to her grandmother's home—right next door to the Congregational church.

"My dear May, I've been holding breakfast for you. You must be hungry after such a long trip," Grandmother Merriam said in greeting, keeping herself at arm's length from the young woman.

May had to resist throwing herself into the tiny woman's arms. Her grandmother was just as she remembered her. Her black cap perched on her head, her white apron starched just so. Not a hair was out of place. No, her grandmother would not appreciate such an impulsive gesture as a big hug. She had never known quite what to do about her impetuous granddaughter.

As soon as the awkward moment passed, grandmother and granddaughter settled down to a bountiful meal. May was amazed at the homemade biscuits, eggs, and bacon, all prepared expertly. Her grandmother seemed so frail at times, yet she was perfectly capable of keeping a beautiful, spotless home and preparing a sumptuous table.

Brushing aside her granddaughter's compliments, the older woman launched into what would be her favorite subject during the course of May's visit: the new young minister. "It's Monday morning so he should be dropping by very soon," she announced casually.

"Dropping by?" May exclaimed. She couldn't believe that her visit was off to such an abysmal start. First she had been jolted by the news that the wonderful elderly minister was gone. How she had loved those buggy rides with all the children in town! She had liked that minister, but she had no desire to become acquainted with the new one. Besides, she had heard about the handsome lawyers who lived on the other side of the church. Maybe she would just go for a leisurely stroll while what's-his-name was visiting Grandmother. . . .

"Why, yes. Oh, don't look so surprised, dear. He enjoys hearing my opinion on matters related to the church and community. Oh, yes. He has taken my advice to heart on many occasions. Let's just clean up these breakfast things, and I'll start a fresh pot of tea for Reverend Sheldon."

69

After helping her grandmother, May went upstairs with her suitcases. She wanted to unpack her dresses, but she also wanted to be alone with her thoughts. How many times would she have to endure this Reverend Sheldon? She had plans to stay in Waterbury for a month. She'd have to start making excuses, and they would have to be good ones. Her grandmother could see through most ruses, she thought with a pang in her heart.

When she returned to the parlor, May saw her grandmother sitting in her familiar rocker, waiting expectantly for her visitor. "There's something you should know about Reverend Sheldon, May," she began. "I like him very much, but he's not like most young men."

May couldn't imagine what that meant. "What do you mean, Grandmother?"

"I just don't want you to be hurt if he ignores you altogether. He isn't being rude. He's just maintaining his image."

May had the sudden urge to burst out laughing. The last thing she wanted was the undivided attention of some pale-faced pastor! "Image?" she queried politely.

"That of the wise young minister, dear. He doesn't want to offend the young women in the church by becoming friendly with any one of them. If he showed one special attention, why, she might make a great deal of trouble for him, and that wouldn't be proper for a man of God."

May knew her grandmother was watching her above

her wire-rimmed spectacles, trying to gauge her reaction. "Well, Grandmother, do not worry about me," May stated rather grandly. "I am not interested in capturing the attention of a minister, especially one with such lofty ideals." Her words, while laced with sarcasm, seemed to have little effect on her grandmother.

At that moment the front doorbell rang, and May felt the bells reverberate in the pit of her stomach. Why couldn't she have escaped somewhere, upstairs or outside, while she had the chance? Now she was trapped in the parlor, like the proverbial fly, waiting to be devoured by the spider.

"I think he has come," Grandmother Merriam said quietly.

For May, that would be the understatement of her life.

In the weeks to come May would relive that moment over and over again. How his frame had filled Grandmother's doorway, how his eyes had met hers and then quickly darted away, how his voice conveyed such concern for his wise old friend Mrs. Merriam.

From his looks, May knew he had to be Scotch-Irish. He was at least six feet tall, with thick dark hair, blue eyes under dark lashes and brows—black Irish, wasn't that the term she had heard?—and a good sturdy chin. His shoulders were exceedingly broad, leading her to imagine that he must be quite an athlete. May had never met any man like him—or any man

71

less interested in her at first meeting.

His smile for her was pleasant enough, but Reverend Charles Sheldon was clearly intent on conversing with Grandmother Merriam. Turning his body in his chair slightly toward the elderly woman, he would rarely direct comments to May, and those few remarks were awkward at best.

"Have you noticed that I haven't performed a funeral service lately?" he asked Mrs. Merriam.

"Good heavens, yes. May, I believe I wrote you about our tragic predicament here in Waterbury. Folks can be so close-minded!"

Charles did his best to suppress a smile, remembering his friend's adamant stand on funeral protocol. "And have you seen my vegetable garden lately? Perhaps you and, er, Miss Merriam would like to stop by? Mother Barrett says she's never seen such beautiful cauliflower."

Soon the conversation became more comfortable, May noticed, as if she weren't even in the parlor. Grandmother Merriam extended yet another invitation to him to join them later in the week for Boston baked beans—a favorite of his—and to inquire about his tennis game, of all things.

"Have you resolved your difficulty with Deacon Adams yet? How he can criticize you for this most trivial matter, I'll never understand," Mrs. Merriam pronounced stiffly.

"Yesterday he reiterated his position again to me

following the worship service, supposedly in confidence, but we were in the presence of other deacons. Something about it wasn't the 'Christian thing' for a minister to play tennis!"

Grandmother Merriam then explained the situation to May, whose face by this time bore a resemblance to a question mark. "Reverend Sheldon has taken to playing tennis every day with those young lawyers in the governor's house. It's late in the afternoon—too late for visiting—and he enjoys the physical activity. If I were young, I'd want to play, too!" she said, laughing delightedly.

At that moment, May gave Charles her most sympathetic look, one that he acknowledged but, again, only briefly.

Clearing his throat, Charles went on to the next topic on his unwritten agenda. "Mrs. Merriam, I've wanted to discuss with you the possibility of selling Pony Bly."

In a flash May's face changed from sympathy to outrage. How could he think of selling that dear, dear animal? And to think she had been on his side a moment earlier. Still, she held her tongue, not wanting to offend her grandmother.

"Reverend Sheldon, this is not a time to feel sentimental. Not many in Waterbury know the real condition of Pony Bly—or if they do, they're not willing to admit it. But I'll come right out and say it: You were sold a bill of goods with that animal." Mrs. Merriam threw May a warning look, and May wisely kept her silence.

"Well, I don't know if I would say that exactly, but the pony is quite ill, it's true. Still, his nervous condition certainly hasn't affected his appetite," he said, laughing.

"May remembers Pony Bly from her earlier visits and all the fun she and the children had riding in the buggy. My dear," Mrs. Merriam said, addressing May, "Reverend Sheldon must pay for the pony's upkeep from his own salary, which is hardly enough to pay for his own needs." Again, Grandmother Merriam threw her granddaughter a warning look. This time May was more puzzled than chastised.

When Reverend Sheldon rose to beg her grand-mother's leave, May realized that nothing had been decided during their morning get-together. They had simply enjoyed each other's company. Besides, she told herself, every minister needs a sympathetic ear.

That evening as grandmother and granddaughter sat with their handwork on their laps, their efforts lighted by kerosene lamps, May caught her grandmother giving her a curious look.

"What is it, Grandmother? Can I get you something?"

The white-haired woman shook her head slightly, and then bowed her head to continue her stitching. But now May was curious.

"It's my needlework, isn't it? Mother says I'll never keep a proper house the way I'm going. I just don't have the patience for stitching!" she added, exasperated, her dark curls shaking and spilling over her forehead. She looked to her grandmother for advice, but the older woman appeared not to be listening at all. "Grandmother, are you all right?" May asked suddenly, her voice etched with concern.

Grandmother's eyes seem to cloud over as a contented smile came over her face.

"Although our minister has a horse and buggy, he has never taken a young lady in Waterbury for a ride. Did I mention that, dear?"

That night—May's first back in Waterbury—she lay awake for a while before drifting off to sleep. Was Grandmother trying to warn her not to accept any invitations from the handsome young pastor? Well, Grandmother needn't worry, May thought, because there won't be any for me to refuse. But if there were. . . what would she say?

Reverend Sheldon found many occasions to visit Mrs. Merriam and May during the weeks that followed. There were Monday morning teas, evening meals with Boston baked beans, and front-yard chats as he was passing by.

Pretty soon May had a good idea of all the town improvements that had come about, thanks to the young pastor. She couldn't walk by the library without thinking of his reading club; she couldn't saunter down Main Street without thinking about its once dusty state. She was amazed that, when faced with an obstacle or predicament, he never doubted that he could overcome it.

She also had discovered a bit about his past, especially his years in the Dakota Territory. She marveled at how difficult life was on the prairie and how much he and his family had managed to overcome. *I can see where his strength of will comes from,* she found herself thinking. *He doesn't want to encourage any girl because he's waiting for the right one, much like he had to wait for good things to happen on the homestead.*

Thanks to her grandmother's constant commentary, May also knew the young pastor couldn't support a wife and family on his small salary. *Grandmother is always on guard for "her" pastor,* May lovingly reflected. *She doesn't want anyone to break his heart!*

Like any vibrant young woman, May was desperate for social interaction. Her grandmother had encouraged her to attend the reading club during her stay, and May had enjoyed going. There were many young men and women her age in Waterbury and the surrounding countryside, and she felt they were all rather cultured. Certainly they were more sophisticated than the young people in her own town—and more fun, too. She had even formed a close friendship with a young woman whom May decided would make a perfect minister's wife. But this particular friend wasn't the only attractive woman with designs on the new pastor. *There are many who would jump at the chance to sit in the buggy with him,* she mused often to herself.

Maybe Grandmother's vigil isn't for naught.

One pleasant summer evening, Grandmother Merriam decided to have a party for May and all her new acquaintances. Naturally, Reverend Sheldon was invited, too, and he arrived alone as expected. After enjoying light refreshments and conversation, the guests began to leave, stopping by the rocking chair to offer their congratulations to Mrs. Merriam on such a successful evening. When the last of the guests had departed, Charles was still there, lingering near May as if waiting to have her full attention. When he noticed Grandmother Merriam go into the kitchen with some cups, he cleared his throat.

"Miss Merriam, since it's such a lovely evening. . .I, er, well, I wondered if you might like to join me for a buggy ride."

"But I understand you have never taken a young lady for a drive," May heard herself saying almost without thinking. "Isn't it against your principles?"

"Yes, that is true," he answered rather nervously. "But you see, I had not met you when I decided to take such a stand."

May felt torn. She couldn't deny her attraction to Reverend Sheldon, but she also didn't want to be the one responsible for ruining his long-cultivated reputation. Before she knew it, she had agreed to go.

Rushing into the kitchen to tell her grandmother, May blurted out the news. Grandmother dried her hands and faced May, her eyes unwavering.

"I fear he has been unwise," she said simply.

May couldn't help but feel a sense of shame as Charles guided Pony Bly down Main Street. She kept her gaze straight ahead, hoping that, under cover of semidarkness, their infamous ride would go unnoticed. Unfortunately, Pony Bly was not willing to be part of such a subterfuge. His nervous condition, referred to by her grandmother, caused the pony to periodically kick the dashboard noisily, causing anyone nearby to look in the direction of the buggy. Occasionally May stole a look at her handsome driver, but his face betrayed no sense of guilt or remorse. Only she wished that this seemingly pleasant ride would soon come to an end.

"I have enjoyed this immensely," Charles said when he at last walked her to her grandmother's door. "I hope you will go with me again."

May thanked him as well and hurried inside. Her face felt flushed from the excitement of the evening. At least, she reminded herself as she went upstairs for the night, her visit was almost over. After she left Waterbury, she would never see Charles Sheldon again.

For the rest of her visit, May Merriam was the object of great interest in Waterbury, Vermont. She could feel the penetrating gazes of churchgoers at the Congregational church; she could almost hear the whispers in the local stores. Her girlfriends, whom she had invited to her party, now treated her differently.

Reverend Sheldon had asked her if she wished to take a second buggy ride, but her common sense prevailed. May couldn't imagine living through another ride, tainting the good pastor's reputation with every mile! Her grandmother seemed especially relieved that she had refused.

"May, dear, you simply are not serious enough to become a pastor's wife," she admonished the young woman. "You were wise not to encourage him further."

May shook her head. "No, Grandmother, Reverend Sheldon won't want a serious wife," she said almost sadly. "He's seen too much that is serious in his life. But you needn't worry. I wouldn't marry a minister if he were the only man left in the world!"

On the day of her departure, May said a brief goodbye to Charles, kissed her grandmother for the last time, and boarded the stagecoach for home. She had plenty to think about on her three-hour journey. She thought of the young lawyers, who had seemed quite interested in her, of her girlfriends, her protective grandmother, and, of course, of Charles Sheldon.

Someday he'll probably take other girls out in his buggy, May thought ruefully. *Anyone who looks like he does—oh, those Scotch-Irish looks!—will want a wife and will get one. Anyone who looks like he does. . .*

She couldn't bring herself to finish that sentence. Shaking herself, May thought, *He's not very practical and he'll never save his money. Ah, well, I'm glad I met him anyway.*

When the stagecoach deposited her at the gate of her home, her mother and father were waiting for her, her mother picking flowers in the yard. As her father helped May with her satchel, he asked, rather casually, "Did you like the new minister in Waterbury?" Uncharacteristically, he seemed to be waiting anxiously for her answer.

May didn't want to seem interested in a man she would never see again. Besides, her father had his eye on a local businessman as his future son-in-law. "No, not much, Father," she replied.

But anyone with such Scotch-Irish looks, indeed, anyone who was waiting for the right woman to take for a buggy ride, was worth another chance.

six

Topeka, Kansas, 1889

W here wagon trains had once congregated before departing for points west, Charles Sheldon would find himself on the first Sunday of the new year in 1889. He was about to begin a new pastorate in a new church in Topeka, Kansas, a city just over thirty years old. It was a position he had only dreamed about, and one that would not have been realized without assistance from an unlikely source.

Before departing for Topeka, Everet Merriam himself had traveled to Waterbury to say good-bye to his aged mother. Like his daughter, he was regaled with many stories about the new pastor, and like her, he found himself seated in one of the front pews of the Congregational church, a copy of the day's sermon in his hand.

Not wanting to upset her father, May had refrained from talking about Reverend Sheldon except when asked, and she certainly hadn't volunteered any information about his sermon style. Surprised and moved by what he heard, Everet returned home favorably impressed. *Here is a young man going places,* he thought, *but he won't get too far if he stays in Waterbury.*

Charles had actually come to the same conclusion himself. While he was devoted to his congregation, and they to him, there were several instances when he found his hands tied. He could not convince the congregation that the member/parish concept was outdated. Neither could he hope to eliminate the selling of church pews. He found the funeral protocol hopelessly impractical and meaningless but bound for better or worse in tradition. Furthermore, the role of the proper minister in a New England community was not one he could play for long. He was an active man, now thirty-one years old, and he could think of no reason why he shouldn't be able to play tennis and enjoy other physical pursuits when he had no other pressing responsibilities.

When Everet Merriam finally moved his family to Topeka at the end of the summer in 1888, one of the first orders of business was finding a new church. Although the First Congregational Church was a distance away, the new residents felt comfortable there. The city was growing at such a rapid pace, though, that soon plans were considered to begin a new Sunday school near Washburn College, in the western reaches of the city, closer to the Merriams' new home. By the end of 1888, this Sunday school had sprouted into a healthy congregation, now known as Central Congregational Church. However, it did not have a full-time minister.

Everet Merriam had just the man in mind for the job. In short order, Charles was invited to Topeka to deliver a sermon at First Church, one that was well received by both congregations. The vote to invite him was unanimous.

After resigning from the Congregational church of Waterbury in November, much to the dismay of his congregants, Charles Sheldon arrived at the one-time threshold to the American frontier. He had left a part of his heart in Vermont, there was no doubt. How could he ever forget the devotion of Mrs. Merriam, the Ladies' Aid Society, the young men and women who flocked to the reading club, and those who gave what they could to support his latest brainstorms?

Yes, he had left part of his heart there, but his mind was racing ahead. The "Golden City" was the place for a man who wanted to change the world.

While the sunlit rolling hills with their colorful autumn elms gave the city its moniker, Topeka was fast becoming a golden city for other reasons. The hub of the Santa Fe Railroad because of its central location in the state, not to mention the cattle and wheat farms surrounding the city, Topeka was also the state capital and boasted many impressive buildings. The days of conflict for the city, known as the "Bleeding Kansas" debacle of the 1850s, which pitted antislavery and proslavery factions against each other, were over. Topeka in 1889 boasted wide avenues lined with prosperous homes. Church spires and trees dotted the landscape like exclamation points.

When Charles arrived in January, the forty members of Central Congregational Church were meeting in a room on the second floor of a meat market. A stone foundation had been laid for a new church, about a block away, but with winter in progress, work would likely not be completed until summer. There was no pulpit in the meeting room and only a barely functional reed organ, but to the new minister none of that mattered. *It's as if I'm in the upper room,* he thought. *The Spirit of God is surely here.*

Later Charles would write, "It is astonishingly true that the Spirit of God pays very little attention to the particular places in which men find Him. It would be interesting to know how many souls have been born again out of doors instead of in temples made with men's hands."

For several months the new pastor labored in these humble surroundings while enjoying the hospitality of Everet Merriam and his family, who had insisted he room with them until he could find his own quarters. As always, money remained a concern for Charles, even with an increase in pay. He was now making one thousand dollars a year, a modest amount even in 1889.

He had to admit he felt rather awkward living in the home of the only woman he had ever invited out on a buggy ride. May felt uncomfortable, too. As the weeks passed, her father, who had extended the open-ended invitation, became anxious for the young minister to leave his home as well. He didn't want to encourage Charles and May's relationship, one that had already budded despite his best intentions.

A few months later, much to Charles's delight, Stewart and Sarah Sheldon and their daughters joined him in Topeka after selling their home in Salem, and he promptly moved in with them. Topeka would be his parents' final home.

On June 23, 1889, the new home of Central Congregational Church was dedicated, with Charles Monroe Sheldon officiating in the pulpit. Reverend Sheldon set the tone for his ministry by proclaiming that this church would preach "a Christ for the common people." He went on to say that this Jesus whom he loved "knows no sect or age, whose religion does not consist alone in cushioned seats, and comfortable surroundings, or culture, or fine singing or respectable orders of Sunday services, but a Christ Who bids us all recognize the Brotherhood of the race, who bids throw open this room to all. . . ."

The next winter Charles would come to understand the plight of the common people in an unusual way. An economic depression was affecting the region, made all the worse by horrific weather conditions. Record snowfalls and plunging temperatures had forced companies out of business and people out of work. When a man came to the door of the church asking for work, Charles could not offer him anything except his heartfelt best wishes.

Years later, likely rectifying his behavior through his fictional minister Philip Strong, Charles would offer what should have been his response to the man at his door:

> *There was nothing remarkable about him. He was poorly dressed and carried a small bundle. He looked cold and tired. Philip, who never could resist the mute appeal of distress in any form, reached out his hand and said kindly, "Come in, my brother, you look cold and weary. Come in and sit down before the fire and we'll have a bite of lunch."*

Charles found himself thinking about that unemployed fellow more and more. What did he, a simple pastor, really know about finding a job? What if he had nothing and had to find work—would anyone hire him? Dressed as a man down and out on his luck with few resources, Charles decided to find out firsthand.

For one week during the brutal winter of 1890, Charles conducted his experiment. His ragged coat flailing in the bitter blasts, his worn leather boots stomping along the ice-crusted streets, Charles began making inquiries in a feed store. The man behind the counter did not even look up from his newspaper to acknowledge Charles's presence, let alone answer his question. Charles politely repeated his query, and this time received a snort as a reply.

"Job! You tell me where I can get one. There isn't business here to keep a hen busy," the man retorted.

Moving on down Kansas Avenue, Topeka's main thoroughfare, Charles stopped in at every store where he was willing to accept employment (tobacco stores and theaters excluded, for moral reasons). At shoe stores, restaurants, hotels, and grocery and hardware stores the answer was the same: There are no jobs now. As the day wore on, and his hands and legs became numb with cold, Charles realized that his was not a true experiment. In the back of his mind he knew he could return to his parents' home for a hearty, warm dinner and a comfortable bed. Still, he thought, the world is a very cold and dreary place where a man who wants to work cannot find a place to do it.

For three more days Charles wandered the streets of Topeka, searching for work. During that time he saw only a few of his parishioners, and as far as he could tell, no one recognized their pastor disguised as a poor man. Finally, midway through the fourth day,

Charles found himself on the tracks of the Santa Fe Railroad. It had been snowing all week and men were hard at work shoveling the snow off the railroad ties and clearing the switches. Charles felt he could almost taste work, so desperately did he desire a job.

When he asked one of the workers what he was making, he was astounded to learn it was $1.75 for the day. After four and a half days, that seemed like an amazingly large sum. Finally, Charles approached one of the men and asked if he could shovel with them, for no pay. No one voiced an objection, and so, borrowing a shovel from a nearby coal yard, Charles set to work. He couldn't believe the thrill he felt, just knowing he was wanted, just to be in the company of human beings who were working. In many ways he was reminded of the joy he had known working on the prairie side by side his father and his brother, often in the midst of a raging storm.

The next day, when he returned the shovel to the coal yard, he received, at last, an offer of work for pay. The man who had lent him the shovel needed someone to shovel coal out of a train car into his bins. Charles jumped at the chance, and by noon had completed the task. He had made fifty cents. After purchasing a cup of coffee and a sandwich, he walked home through another blizzard, the remaining forty cents jangling in his pocket. He couldn't wait until Sunday—the next day—to tell his congregation all about his experiences.

At the Sunday evening service, after describing his adventures, he launched almost breathlessly into his next plan, one that had evolved from what had happened during the week. The idea was similar to his "boarding around" concept carried out so successfully in Waterbury. This time, though, instead of getting better acquainted with families, Charles wanted to know Topeka better as a community.

"I have divided Topeka into eight groups of people," he began. "There are streetcar operators, college students, Negroes, railroad workers, lawyers, physicians, businessmen, and newspaper workers. I'll spend a whole week with each of these groups, living the life they live, asking them questions about their work," he explained. "Most important, I'll be preaching the gospel to them in whatever way seems best."

Charles was on the frontier of a ministry so exciting and fulfilling that nothing else would consume him for some time. Like his fictional protagonist Philip Strong, Charles felt he was living in "an age that calls for heroes, martyrs, servants, [and] saviors."

The first week, as planned, Charles could be found riding the streetcars from one end of Topeka to the other. A rather costly endeavor, he soon found he had spent all his loose change, but he did have the chance to talk with the motormen and conductors. They were proud of the fact that Topeka boasted the longest electric streetcar line in the entire Midwest, but they had real concerns about their wages, housing conditions, and spiritual condition.

Washburn College, founded in 1865, was the focus of the pastor's second week, one that he thoroughly enjoyed. He attended classes with the students, played games with the baseball team in the indoor gymnasium, and tried to fit in as best he could with campus life. In particular, Charles wanted to discover as much as he could about the religious life of the college. What was the teachers' definition of religion, and how were they perpetuating their ideas in their courses?

The third week would be the most pivotal of all, and it soon became apparent to Charles that one week was not enough. He would end up spending three weeks with the blacks of Topeka—referred to as Negroes at the time—in the segregated section of Topeka known as Tennesseetown. Few white men ventured into Tennesseetown. About one thousand freed slaves and their children lived in the settlement, which was only a few blocks from Central Congregational Church.

The first week he spent trying to understand the depths of their poverty and helping a few men to secure jobs. Unemployment was extremely high in Tennesseetown as few businesses were willing to hire blacks for anything except the most menial tasks. Following that pitifully brief foray as a missionary, Charles spent a second week visiting black schools. Finally, he spent some time with the leading citizens of the black community. He also engaged in a social experiment to determine the extent of racism in Topeka.

On one occasion, he and a black man entered a

restaurant and shared a table. Both were served without question. Then, he and the black man entered another restaurant separately. Again, both were served, much to Charles's surprise. Finally, Charles accompanied the black man to the local YMCA (Young Men's Christian Association) where the latter applied for membership. This time he was refused, on the basis of his color.

To Charles, the weeks spent in and out of Tennesseetown planted the seeds of a new mission for his church. It would take a while for his plans to be implemented, but he was now seeing Topeka with the blinders off. He had seen a need so great and so desperate that he could not sit by and do nothing.

Charles's experiment continued during his next week on the railroad. To him this was the most enjoyable time of all as he was given permission to play a more active role. For the entire week he had a pass to ride any train, passenger or freight, and on any engine of any train, coming into or going out of Topeka. He could ride as far east as Kansas City and as far west as Emporia. He spent two exciting nights riding the caboose, and twice he jumped from one car to another when the train was in motion. More importantly to his mission, he was able to converse freely with brakemen, conductors, and even engineers on occasion.

When he visited with the town's lawyers, he was given free rein to attend court sessions, and he also spent time reading cases and discussing briefs with the attorneys. Charles found himself poring over law journals in the evening, trying to prepare for the next day. Before spending a week with the physicians, he secured permission from the local president of Topeka's medical association to attend the association's weekly meeting and have access to the hospitals. He thus was allowed to observe operations and go on rounds and make house calls with doctors, too. The seventh week he spent with Topeka's businessmen, visiting with them in their places of business. Charles felt that week to be his least successful and, in general, least interesting.

But his last week would not be dull. As an unpaid reporter for the Topeka *Daily Capital,* Charles was given a beat of his own: covering transportation, hotels, and the suburbs. He came to understand the workings of a daily newspaper, and at the same time, its myriad shortcomings, as he saw them. From his week immersed in the town's print media, Charles concluded that what was needed was a Christian newspaper, run and written by Christians, that was committed to uplifting the community. (Years later, he would be given the opportunity to bring his idea to fruition. No one, it seemed, could deny Charles Sheldon when faced with his contagious goodwill and enthusiasm.)

Every Sunday during his experiment brought new faces to Central Congregational Church. They were there because Charles had invited them, men and women beside whom he had personally labored during the week. Many returned Sunday after Sunday to hear a preacher like none they had ever known. As Charles

Sheldon had promised, this church was one where "a Christ for the common people" was proclaimed, and proclaimed with unmitigated joy.

On May 20, 1891, a joyous celebration of another sort took place at Central Congregational Church. On that day Charles Monroe Sheldon and Mary Abby Merriam were joined in holy matrimony after a sporadic courtship. Their union, which would last until death parted them, would be intensely private. Neither Charles nor May kept a diary or was fond of sharing personal anecdotes in public.

Glimpses into the couple's private life can be seen, however, in Charles's novels, which were often auto-biographical in nature. In *The Crucifixion of Philip Strong* there is this telling exchange:

> *"What do you think of that, Sarah?" asked Philip Strong as he finished the letter.*
>
> *"Two thousand dollars is twice as much as we are getting now, Philip."*
>
> *"What! You mercenary little creature, do you think of the salary first?"*
>
> *"If I did not think of it once in a while I doubt if you would have a decent meal or a good suit of clothes," replied the minister's wife, looking at him with a smile.*

Several pages later, the couple tangles humorously

over Philip's ministerial style, a likely topic of conversation between the newlyweds:

"Only, dear Philip, be wise. Do not try to reform everything in a week; or expect people to grow their wings before they have started even pin feathers. It isn't natural."

"Well, I won't," replied Philip with a laugh. "Better trim your wings, Sarah. They're dragging on the floor."

Not everyone shared completely in the joy of the moment at the wedding. May's outgoing personality had not endeared her to Stewart and Sarah Sheldon, who may have agreed with the elderly Mrs. Merriam's assessment of the proper minister's wife. At the same time, May's father, who had become a very successful banker in Topeka, didn't quite approve of Charles's "get acquainted" schemes and zealous efforts to build up the church. Charles, writing again in Philip Strong, would agree with his father-in-law wholeheartedly:

"Yes," said Philip simply. "I am. . .impulsive and impractical, but heart and soul and body and mind I simply want to do the will of God. Is it not so?"

"I know it is," she said, "and if you go to Milton it will be because you want to do His will more than to please yourself."

94

Nonetheless, Everet Merriam was a generous man when it came to his beloved daughter, and as a wedding gift, he built the couple their first home—near the church, of course.

That was a good thing for Charles, who would spend practically every waking moment over the next several years devoted to his all-encompassing ministry. After the wedding, his most immediate concern would be found almost right at his front door. Tennesseetown was, after all, just a stone's throw away.

seven

If Charles Sheldon had shaken up Topeka by spending three weeks in Tennesseetown during his so-called experiment, he now was ready for an encore that would make that performance pale in comparison. Moreover, he was fully prepared to shake up Tennesseetown itself, a task that to him was long overdue.

In so doing, he hoped to better both races, black and white. "I do not have much hope of Christianizing the Negro," he wrote in a local publication at the time, "until we have Christianized the Anglo-Saxon. It is a present question with me now, sometimes, which race needs it more." Charles would again express his feelings in a sermon given by the fictional minister Philip Strong:

"I do not believe the work of this church
consists in having so many meetings and
socials and pleasant gatherings and delightful
occasions among its own members. But the
real work of this church consists in getting out
of its own little circle. . .and going in any way
most effective to the world's wounded, to bind
up the hurt and be a savior to the lost."

When the Compromise of 1877 effectively ended the Reconstruction period following the American Civil War, freed slaves in large numbers began heading North in search of a better life. There were numerous advertisements offering cheap land to be had in the western United States, land that was just a train ride away. Desperate to begin new lives, these former slaves boarded the rails, only to be turned away in such hubs as St. Louis and Kansas City. Wandering farther west, many eventually found a home in Topeka. By 1880, more than forty thousand freed slaves had passed through Topeka, and three thousand chose to settle there.

They and their children may have found a home, but they were far from welcome. The racism described by Charles in his novel *The Redemption of Freetown*, a thinly veiled account of his work in Tennesseetown, was undoubtedly not far from the truth:

"Why, who else could have done it, doctor?" exclaimed Isabel excitedly. "We all know the colored people have done just such things repeatedly. They are simply awful. They ought to be punished. I for one believe they were a good deal better off in slavery. It's where they belong."

"Isabel!" said Mr. Vernon.

"It's what I believe. The miserable creatures! Of what use are they?"

"I feel the same," cried Winifred. "I think every Negro in Freetown ought to be transported to Africa, so we could get Merton forever rid of them."

In *The Crucifixion of Philip Strong,* Charles described a neighborhood similar to Topeka's seamiest section:

There are two feeble mission schools which are held in plain, unattractive halls, where every Sunday a handful of children meet. But nothing practically is being done by the church of Christ in this place to give the people in that part of the town the privileges and power of the life of Christ, the life more abundantly. The houses down there are of the cheapest description. The people who come out of them are far from well dressed. The

streets and alleys are dirty and ill-smelling.
And no one cares to promenade for pleasure
up and down the sidewalk in that neighbor-
hood. It is not a safe place to go to at night.
The most frequent disturbances come from
that part of town. All the hard characters find
refuge there.

Indeed, Tennesseetown was characterized by high crime, high unemployment, and desperate poverty, not to mention a disreputable establishment known as Jordan Hall. Named for its owner, Andy Jordan, the illegal speakeasy soon became a target for Charles Sheldon. First, though, the determined pastor had to become better acquainted with the residents of Topeka's only ghetto.

To do that, Charles asked a Presbyterian minister to accompany him every other Monday night to deliver lectures that he felt would be of interest to the community. They would be speaking in one of Tennesseetown's four churches, the Tennesseetown Congregational Church. These churches were not grand structures of the kind built in downtown Topeka. Rather they were humble buildings, barely distinguishable from the shacks that dotted street after street in the settlement. Charles and Reverend Harris lectured on such diverse topics as "One Dollar and What It Can Buy," "Light," "A Quart of Whisky and What It Can Do," and "What Has Been Done for the Negro Since the War."

Men and boys in great numbers turned out to hear the two ministers, and soon Charles began to know many of them. In a few weeks, Charles decided to pay house calls on those he knew by name, the first time for many black families that a white man had entered their homes. In a few weeks, Charles, like the fictional Reverend Howard Douglass in *The Redemption of Freetown,* had reached a conclusion:

> *How shall we redeem Freetown? It is not an impossibility. It is not a vague dream of what may be. It is within the reach of actual facts. It can be redeemed. The place can be saved, even as a soul by itself can be saved by Jesus. But it is God's way to save men by means of other men. He does not save by means of angels, or in any way apart from the use of men as the means. What will you do to redeem Freetown? I have a plan. I want you to listen to it.*

From his visits and those made by other members of his church, Charles determined that among the many needs of Tennesseetown, the greatest was the lack of a kindergarten. He also selected the most feasible location for the school since none of the churches would be adequate. In all of the rag-tag settlement, he could find no better facility than the infamous Jordan Hall.

After negotiations with Andy Jordan were conducted,

a most surprising agreement was reached: Jordan Hall would be leased to Central Congregational Church for the next two years! When Stewart Sheldon, his eyebrows raised, asked how the arrangement came about, Charles was unfazed. "I simply offered him more money that he could make," he replied. To Charles, money was simply another obstacle that a little fundraising could overcome.

From the summer of 1892 until the kindergarten officially opened in the spring of 1893, the tireless minister and his congregants threw themselves into generating the necessary funds and restoring Jordan Hall. "They walked and ran into places where angels were hard to find," Charles wrote years later as he sought to describe his congregation's efforts. "Their very ignorance of the problems involved over in Tennesseetown made them immune to fear or defeat. . . . The entire prospect was without hope of reward or success. But when once the picture of what might be done was clear to them they threw themselves into the adventure as eagerly and courageously as any missionary force in any foreign land."

The actual work was described in *The Redemption of Freetown,* where Reverend Douglass and his church undertook a similar project. Costing between two thousand and three thousand dollars—an accurate reflection of what Charles paid to Mr. Jordan—the renovated dance hall contained a "day-nursery for the babies of the mothers who are obliged to go away from home all day to labor, a kitchen where cooking can be taught, bathrooms, a reading-room, smaller rooms for classes in sewing or music, a dispensary, an office, and a basement fitted for teaching trades."

On April 3, 1893, the kindergarten opened in the newly renovated (and renamed) Union Hall. For the next two years Andy Jordan's dance hall would never be the same.

Already in his short ministry Charles Sheldon had established a pattern: He had seen a need in his community and he had filled it. From the start the Tennesseetown kindergarten was a success as mothers and fathers started bringing their children in droves to the Union Hall school. By 1900, seven years later, a total of 287 children had attended the kindergarten.

For the first two years the school remained in Union Hall before relinquishing the facility back to its owner. During that time, plans were underway to renovate Tennesseetown Congregational Church so that the school could move there when the lease expired. The school remained at the church for the next sixteen years until the city of Topeka officially began supporting kindergartens and the Tennesseetown kindergarten was incorporated into a local public school.

Charles acted like a proud father when, several years after the school started, an exhibit put together by the kindergarten won prizes at two expositions. In 1904 at the St. Louis World's Fair, the children's arts exhibit won second prize in a national contest. Then, in 1907, at the Jamestown Tercentennial Exposition, the Tennesseetown kindergarten—then known as the Sheldon Kindergarten so as not to give the impression that the school was from the state of Tennessee—was awarded the silver medal.

Obviously, Charles could not take full credit for the school, but he was more than pleased by the personnel the church had hired to be in charge, financed largely by white businessmen in Topeka. Under the direction of head teacher June Chapman, table manners and cleanliness became topics of discussion along with the ABCs. A mothers' group—known as the Sheldon League of American Mothers—began meetings held along the lines of the modern PTA. During summers, kindergartners began developing their own gardens, much as their founder had done in Vermont. A student band of cornet players was also formed, and those children delighted in learning marches to perform for special occasions.

During the time that the kindergarten occupied Union Hall, a member of his congregation gave Charles a suggestion. Since the church held the lease on the building, why not make use of the hall at night as well? Charles couldn't help remembering his situation at Waterbury, even though the circumstances were different in Tennesseetown. After conferring with staff members and broaching the idea with the church's college students, Charles decided to start a library in the classrooms of Union Hall, to be open only during the evenings.

Charles had obtained the support of the college students for a reason. He wanted them to staff the library, and they had all agreed enthusiastically. Now there was only one pressing need: books. "Instead of asking for money, books are a pleasant change," he announced from the pulpit. "So I've decided to hold a social evening at the church next Saturday, with the price of admission being one book!"

The social was a huge success, with enough books donated to fill a small library. Even after the library opened in 1894, annual socials were held to replenish the supply and, of course, to provide new and interesting titles. According to a report to the church in *The Redemption of Freetown,* the library committee had supplied the new facility with "magazines, papers, and books." But it had other plans in mind, too: "Besides that, we believe we can carry good papers to the different houses in Freetown, and direct the reading by means of reading-circles, especially in the winter. Our main object, however, will be to help make the new reading-room attractive, and to serve as librarians or attendants different evenings during the week, if Mr. Douglass [the minister] says that is the best way to serve." Despite a few problems with discipline among the patrons, when the kindergarten moved to the church, the library moved as well.

At the time the suggestion for the library was made,

Charles entertained other ideas for Union Hall, as well. On Saturday afternoons, women from Central Congregational began offering sewing classes to the girls and women of Tennesseetown, while the boys received instruction on basket weaving. The boys were particularly happy to learn this skill as they could make a profit selling their creations.

Despite the role of Central Church in the kindergarten, library, and weekend classes, none of these undertakings in Tennesseetown was especially spiritual in nature, a fact deeply troubling to the pastor. A Sunday school had been started in Tennesseetown Congregational Church at about the same time Central Church had moved to its permanent location. While he first offered his services as a bass singer in a visiting quartet, Charles soon began enlisting his members to assist the struggling black church. Attendance at the Sunday school more than doubled during the last ten years of the nineteenth century, and both churches enjoyed a free exchange of ideas, with Tennesseetown residents often sitting in the pews of Central Church for a Sunday evening service.

At the same time, a Christian Endeavor Society chapter was started at the settlement church (one was already thriving at Central Church). These meetings of young people were usually held on Sunday afternoons and were hotbeds of missionary activity. To have an Endeavor society in Tennesseetown, according to Charles, could only spell hope for the future of the black residents of Topeka.

As the years passed, Charles used his influence with his father-in-law and other prominent Topekans to obtain special privileges for the residents of Tennessee-town. Everet Merriam was able to make interest-free loans, while local lawyers and doctors offered free legal and medical assistance to those in need. By 1898, things were beginning to look brighter for many, despite the general appearance of the community. Compared to the rest of Topeka, Tennesseetown still resembled a ghetto, with dirt lawns, garbage strewn about, and few gardens and flowers. To rectify that situation, A. B. Whiting, a deacon, brought his suggestion to Charles.

"We could start a Village Improvement Society," Whiting proposed. "We could even offer prizes as motivation."

Charles mulled over the idea for a few moments. No one could deny that Tennesseetown was in dire need of beautification, but maybe as a church they had already done enough. No one wants a helping hand all the time. "A. B., I think we should let the people of Tennesseetown decide," he said. "If they want a competition, then of course we'll support it."

Even though it was labeled as a plan of Charles Sheldon's, the society was not immediately embraced. As Charles had predicted, there were concerns. One man didn't want whites always telling him how to live; another woman still wanted to keep her hogs on her property, her main source of food in the winter. But in the end, the vote to adopt the garden competition passed.

At a meeting in the spring of 1898 it was decided that prizes would be given for gardening, best-looking home (inside and out), cooking, sewing, as well as several other categories—nine in all. The prizes would consist of cash awards and gifts for the home, all donated by Topeka's merchants. Garden seeds and paint were provided, as well as the necessary tools, and the results were overwhelming, at least to Charles and A. B. Whiting.

"Tennesseetown certainly looks like a different place," A. B. commented at the fall awards ceremony.

Charles had a concerned look on his face. "Still, I don't want this to be another Central Church program," he said.

In a few years, after several successful Village Improvement Society competitions, the leadership roles of the society were given to Tennesseetown residents. Charles felt most pleased at that decision. The latest competition had been covered by the Topeka *Daily Capital* and featured oratory contests, as well as an exhibition of quilts, handcrafts, and homemade baked goods. While Central Church would maintain an auxiliary role in the society—and Charles himself would never miss a contest—Tennesseetown outside and inside was becoming a healed community.

eight

Charles and May's new home had many fine features, but one particularly appealed to Charles: a wonderful, wraparound front porch supported by elegant white pillars and unhindered by screens.

Visitors to the Sheldons' rambling home often remarked on the many and varied styles of windows, including four half-circle shapes that provided dramatic views from all sides, or the different construction materials used (stone for the foundation, wooden beams on the lower half, and cedar shake on the top half). But none of that really mattered to the pastor of Central Church. He needed a place where he could cool off in the summer, a place where he could possibly catch a breeze, if one came his way. He had learned how to endure and thrive in the cruelest winters, but so far he had not mastered the humid, stifling, breezeless Kansas summers when temperatures would often hover in the low 100s.

In the middle of the heat wave of 1896, Charles began his new novel, sitting on the porch of 1515 West 15th Street. *Maybe thinking about September will help me forget about the humidity,* he mused as he sat with pen poised above a sheaf of white papers. He watched as a trickle of perspiration dropped from his cheek onto the unlined paper, and then he quickly wiped his brow with his starched handkerchief.

"Would you care for a glass of lemonade, Charles?" May called to him from inside the screen door.

He nodded his head, too uncomfortable to mumble a reply. But his thoughts were still on that first October Sunday evening when he would face an eager audience, ready to hear chapter 1 of his new book—the one he was about to write. He could picture the fresh-faced Washburn College students, the Ladies' Aid Society, the Christian Endeavor young people, and the deacons and their wives all in attendance.

Five years earlier attendance had been rather pitiful at the Sunday evening service, a trend common in other Topeka churches. Even his father had suggested that Charles might want to discontinue the evening service and throw himself more into planning for

Sunday mornings. But that had only created a challenge in Charles's mind. He could attract people on Sunday evenings; he just had to figure out how.

Finally, he decided that if folks were tired of listening to him preach, perhaps they wouldn't mind if he read them a story. He had always enjoyed when his mother read to him or when Uncle Joe told a dramatic story in his Yankton church. And for Charles, who had never stopped writing since his days on the prairie, the choice of literature was never a problem. He would simply read the sparse congregation his latest effort.

His first story, the novel *Richard Bruce or The Life That Now Is,* was almost an immediate success. Three weeks into the story—Charles read one or more chapters each week—the church was packed. And for those who missed one week, the dedicated pastor would distribute synopses of each chapter. But no one wanted to be away since Charles, ever the crafty writer, ended each chapter at a particularly dramatic moment. Furthermore, he had planned his novels carefully so that he began reading after Washburn College was in session and finished a week or so before Christmas, usually a few days before the students went home for the holidays.

From his first success in 1891 came five other stories, each received equally well. Their titles were dramatic and inspiring at the same time: *Robert Hardy's Seven Days,* the story of a man who was told he had only a week to live; *The Twentieth Door; The*

Crucifixion of Philip Strong, a novel of a minister who gave up everything to proclaim the Gospel; *John King's Question Class;* and *His Brother's Keeper,* a tale of a strike in the iron mines of Upper Michigan. (From 1891 until his retirement from the ministry in 1919, Charles would pen thirty novels to be read on Sunday evenings, all of which were eventually published.)

Charles's novels, like other popular "social gospel" literature of the era, contained common themes. They were tributes to the middle-class working man, caught between the simpler days of rural living and the impending industrial modernization of the twentieth century. The differences between the rich and the poor, labor management and the struggling factory workers, and those who frequented barrooms and who were faithful churchgoers were emphasized. But his novels were filled with optimism, too. The future always looked bright whenever the protagonist decided to follow God's way and seek solutions found in the Bible.

Of his decision to tell stories instead of deliver sermons, Charles would write years later, "I found a real mental relief to turn from the sermonic and homiletic style of sermon preparation to the story form. It is true that the love chapter of life can be told in a sermon and preached from a pulpit, but not with the freedom possible in a story, or by the use of fiction to illustrate the theme."

As he sat in his white wicker chair, trying to fan

111

himself with blank sheets of paper, Charles had a title in mind for his seventh selection. Of all the stories, he knew this one would hit the closest to home:

It was Friday morning and the Rev. Henry Maxwell was trying to finish his Sunday morning sermon. He had been interrupted several times and was growing nervous as the morning wore away, and the sermon grew very slowly toward a satisfactory finish.

Charles read again the first two sentences of his new novel, the one he had tentatively titled *In His Steps*. (Hardly coincidentally, the fictional Henry Maxwell would choose as his scriptural text 1 Peter 2:21: "For even hereunto were ye called: because Christ also suffered for us, leaving us an example, that ye should follow his steps.") He knew he was creating a character very much like himself, but there were differences, too. While he and Henry Maxwell were both successful pastors of churches in the American Midwest (Maxwell of a church located in the fictional town of Raymond) and both were married, childless men, Maxwell had become all too used to a comfortable pastorate and a church attended by only the "best people." Central Congregational Church, located near Tennesseetown, was certainly not in the best location in Topeka, nor were its attendees especially well to do. From Charles's Vermont days, his social conscience had distinguished him from other mainstream pastors, but Henry Maxwell's conscience had lain dormant and was about to be awakened for the first time.

Henry's transformation would begin with an encounter much like one Charles had experienced during his early days in Topeka. An unemployed man came to his door—in Henry's case, a tramp—asking for work at the church. Maxwell's response to the man was polite yet firm: He had nothing to offer and besides, he was too busy at the moment. On Sunday, during another of Henry Maxwell's meticulously conceived services, the tramp and the well-groomed pastor would meet again. This time Henry would not be able to ignore the poor man's cry for help:

> *Suddenly, into the midst of this perfect accord and concord between preacher and audience, there came a very remarkable interruption. It would be difficult to indicate the extent of the shock. . . . It came from the rear of the church from one of the seats under the gallery. The next moment the figure of a man came out of the shadow there and walked down the middle aisle. Before the startled congregation fairly realized what was going on the man had reached the open space in front of the pulpit and had turned about facing the people. . . .*
>
> *Mr. Maxwell had not taken his seat, and he*

*now remained standing, leaning on his pulpit,
looking down at the stranger. It was the man
who had come to his house the Friday before,
the same dusty, worn, shabby-looking young
man. He held his faded hat in his two hands. It
seemed to be a favorite gesture. He had not been
shaved and his hair was rough and tangled. It is
doubtful if any one like this had ever confronted
the First Church within the sanctuary.*

The tramp went on to explain that he had lost his
job ten months ago and since then his life had fallen
apart. His wife had died in their filthy tenement, their
one child, a girl, had been sent to live with another
family, and he had traveled all across the country in
search of work:

*"Of course, I understand you can't all go
out of your way to hunt up jobs for other people like me. I'm not asking you to; but what I
feel puzzled about is, what is meant by following Jesus. What do you mean when you sing
'I'll go with Him, with Him, all the way'? Do
you mean that you are suffering and denying
yourselves and trying to save lost, suffering
humanity just as I understand Jesus did?. . . It
seems to me there's an awful lot of trouble in
the world that somehow wouldn't exist if all
the people who sing such songs went and lived*

*them out. I suppose I don't understand. But
what would Jesus do? Is that what you mean
by following His steps? It seems to me sometimes as if the people in the big churches had
good clothes and nice houses to live in, and
money to spend for luxuries, and could go
away on summer vacations and all that, while
the people outside the churches, thousands of
them, I mean, die in tenements, and walk the
streets for jobs, and never have a piano or a
picture in the house, and grow up in misery
and drunkenness and sin."*

Charles put his pen down and rubbed his eyes. The
tramp would have to die within the next week to force
a pastor such as Henry Maxwell to face his congregation with new resolve. So shaken by the events that had
occurred in such a short time, Henry would appear in
the pulpit as never before and utter words that would
have seemed incomprehensible seven days earlier:

*"The appearance and words of this stranger
in the church last Sunday made a very powerful
impression on me. I am not able to conceal
from you or myself the fact that what he said,
followed as it has been by his death in my
house, has compelled me to ask as I never
asked before, 'What does following Jesus
mean?'. . . . What I am going to propose now is*

115

*something which ought not to appear unusual
or at all impossible of execution. . . . I want
volunteers from the First Church who will
pledge themselves, earnestly and honestly for
an entire year, not to do anything without first
asking the question, 'What would Jesus do?'
And after asking that question, each one will
follow Jesus as exactly as he knows how, no
matter what the result may be."*

Immediately after the service, Henry Maxwell
would meet with those interested in carrying out such
a plan. Among the fifty parishioners present at this
meeting and willing to participate in their pastor's
experiment were Alexander Powers, superintendent of
the "great railroad shops"; Donald Marsh, president of
the local Lincoln College; Milton Wright, a prominent
businessman; Dr. West, a well-respected surgeon; Jasper
Chase, a best-selling author; Virginia Page, an heiress;
Rachel Winslow, an up-and-coming singer and member of the church quartet; and Edward Norman, editor
of the Raymond *Daily News*.

Based on Charles's own experiment in Topeka, he
knew who would make good representatives of the
community. He also knew the problems each would
encounter if they did indeed choose to walk "in His
steps." Again, with a nod to his week spent in the
offices of the Topeka *Daily Capital*, Charles decided
to begin chapter 3 with Edward Norman's first true

test as a newspaper editor who was newly committed to Jesus Christ.

Perhaps Charles could picture himself in Ed Norman's shoes, trying to put out a newspaper that Jesus would be proud to read. Pen in hand, Charles found the words flowing out, so keenly was he aware of the workings of the 1896 newsroom. Among the issues Ed Norman would face over the course of one year were whether to print three columns about the result of a prizefight; whether to accept tobacco and liquor advertising; and whether to print the highly lucrative Sunday edition. On all of these issues Ed Norman said no, and in so doing, put the newspaper on the verge of bankruptcy.

Alexander Powers's choices about how Jesus would act as a superintendent of a thriving company created equally distressing consequences. Charles knew the way such businesses often skirted the law, and he was determined to include this in his book. When Powers discovers that the railroad shop has been consistently violating an Interstate Commerce Law, he knows he must act as Jesus would, but he also knows the price he will pay with his family. When he resigns and assumes a lesser position running a telegraph, his wife and daughter refuse to appear in public, so keen is their humiliation:

No one but himself knew the bitterness of that family estrangement and misunderstanding

117

*of the higher motive. Yet many of the disciples
present in the meeting carried similar burdens.
These were things which they could not talk
about. Henry Maxwell, from his knowledge of
his people, could almost certainly know that
obedience to their pledge had produced in the
heart of families separation of sympathy and
even the introduction of enmity and hatred.
Truly, a man's foes are they of his own household when the rule of Jesus is obeyed by some
and disobeyed by others. Jesus is a great
divider of life. One must walk parallel with
Him or directly across His way.*

A few chapters after Powers discovers his company's error, Donald Marsh, president of a local
college much like Washburn, reveals the error of his
professional life, now that he is seeing things from
Jesus' perspective: "I confess with shame that I have
purposely avoided the responsibility that I owe to this
city personally. I understand that our city officials are
a corrupt, unprincipled set of men, controlled in large
part by the whiskey element and thoroughly selfish so
far as the affairs of city government are concerned,"
he states ruefully.

Together with Henry Maxwell, Marsh organizes
the Christian forces of Raymond to battle the saloons,
with mixed results. While they lose the election (their
whiskey-free candidates do not win), their efforts,

chronicled in the editorial pages of the *Daily News,* are not entirely in vain. There is a sense of hope, at last, for the future of a town such as Raymond.

The stories of the women characters become entwined as they search for a deeper meaning to their lives, now that they have pledged to do as Jesus would. Rachel Winslow, a beauty possessed of a remarkable singing voice, must mull over two career moves, both of which would propel her into the national spotlight, as well as two declarations of love from very different men. Virginia Page, the heiress whose life up until now has been lived out in the newspaper's society pages, must decide whether to continue living a comfortable Christian life or to use her money to help others. The interests of the two young women come together at a tent meeting in the Rectangle, the slum and tenement district of Raymond (much like Tennesseetown).

In the end, the two friends answer the question "What would Jesus do?" with appropriate answers: Virginia decides to finance a home for the lost women of the Rectangle, while Rachel pledges to start a music school there, instructing and inspiring others by example. Virginia also agrees to finance a new Christian newspaper, to be run by Ed Norman. Freed from the responsibility of her wealth, Virginia says, "I have come to know lately that the money which I have called my own is not mine, but God's. . . . What have I done with God's money all these years but gratify my own selfish personal desires? What can I do with the rest of it but try to make some reparation for what I have stolen from God? That is the way I look at it now. I believe it is what Jesus would do."

Meanwhile, at the First Church of Raymond, no one can overlook the difference in Henry Maxwell's sermons:

> *There was in it rebuke for sin, especially hypocrisy, there was definite rebuke of the greed of wealth and the selfishness of fashion, two things that First Church never heard rebuked this way before, and there was a love of his people that gathered new force as the sermon went on. When it was finished there were those who were saying in their hearts, "The Spirit moved that sermon." And they were right.*

And then there are the differences in the man himself. Gone is the "self-satisfied, contented, easy attitude of the fine figure and refined face in the pulpit." Henry now possesses "a love, an earnestness, a passion, a desire, a humility" that enables him to deliver sermons and offer prayers that have the ring of sincerity, and the occasional grammatical lapse. Instead of taking the European vacation that he and his wife had been saving for, Henry quietly arranges for a poor family living in the Rectangle to take a summer vacation, the first time the family has ever left their forbidding tenement.

Moreover, Henry Maxwell is used by God to spread the word of his church's radical experiment. At the end of the year, the experiment is well on its way to becoming a movement, and the changed pastor has been invited to speak at one of the largest churches in Chicago:

What is the test of Christian discipleship? Is it not the same as in Christ's own time? Have our surroundings modified or changed the text? If Jesus were here today would He not call some of the members of this very church to do just what He commanded the young man, and ask them to give up their wealth and literally follow Him? I believe He would do that if He felt certain that any church member thought more of his possessions than of the Saviour. The test would be the same to-day as then. I believe Jesus would demand—He does demand now—as close a following, as much suffering, as great self-denial as when He lived in person on the earth and said, "Except a man renounce all that he hath he cannot be my disciple". . .

The call of this dying century and of the new one soon to be, is a call for a new discipleship, a new following of Jesus, more like the early, simple, apostolic Christianity, when the disciples left all and literally followed the Master. Nothing but a discipleship of this kind

can face the destructive selfishness of the age
with any hope of overcoming it.

The weather had begun to change as September arrived, a subtle change that seemed to whisper fall was around the corner. Charles had poured all of himself into this book and now, with a less sultry breeze ruffling his almost completed manuscript, he thought about the ending:

> *His sermon in Chicago finished, and the day at a close, Henry Maxwell, the weary pastor, is about to retire for the night. But then his mind begins to wander and he has a vision of what the future could mean for those at First Church—and for Jesus' followers everywhere.*
> *He rose at last with the awe of one who has looked at heavenly things. He felt the human forces and the human sins of the world as never before. And with a hope that walks hand in hand with faith and love Henry Maxwell, disciple of Jesus, laid him down to sleep and dreamed of the regeneration of Christendom, and saw in his dream a church of Jesus without spot or wrinkle or any such thing, following him all the way, walking obediently in His steps.*

Satisfied, Charles put down his pen and watched

the first fireflies of the evening lighting the front yard. In the weeks to come he would make few changes in his manuscript. He had said what he wanted and what he hoped his congregation would want to hear. Little did he realize he had written a story that millions would want to read.

On Sunday night, October 4, 1896, Charles Sheldon read the first chapter of *In His Steps* to an eager audience. As he imagined, there was a cross-section of his congregation in attendance. And as he desired, they were extremely attentive and appreciative, with many expressing how anxious they were to return the following Sunday.

A few weeks later Charles received a letter in the mail from the Advance Publishing Company in Chicago. May was more curious than Charles when she read the return address.

"What is it, Charles? You'll have to admit, it looks rather important, yes?"

Reading the contents of the letter, Charles couldn't help but look pleased. "They want to publish *In His Steps* in serial form," he said. "And they're willing to pay me seventy-five dollars for the rights!"

"They" referred to *The Advance,* a weekly publication with a circulation of twenty-one thousand that proclaimed in its banner headline, "Published Weekly in the interests of Congregationalism." Clearly, word of Charles's latest effort had spread through denominational channels to the headquarters of this small publication. What was unusual was that *The Advance* was willing to pay anything to a relatively unknown author. (A few years earlier the publication had issued *Robert Hardy's Seven Days* and *The Crucifixion of Philip Strong* in serial form without remuneration.)

May threw her arms around her bewildered husband. "I can't wait to tell Mother and Father," she cried. "They will be so pleased."

Charles shook his head at his wife. He didn't want to remind her that publication in *The Advance* was hardly an indication of success, as evidenced by his previous published stories. However, it was a start.

On November 5, upon securing the rights, *The Advance* issued its first installment (one chapter) of *In His Steps,* with a photograph of the Rev. Charles M. Sheldon on its cover. By December, when Charles had finished reading the novel on Sunday evenings and when readers of *The Advance* were just a short way into the book, the consensus was overwhelmingly favorable. Hardly a day went by that someone didn't tell him that he should get that book published.

"Chicago, that's the place to go," Everet Merriam advised in his most professional tone of voice. "There are several important publishers there, Charles. And just because *The Advance* paid you for serial rights doesn't mean you have to go back there," he added.

May, now seven months' pregnant, seconded her father's idea enthusiastically. With their first child due at the end of February, a little extra money would come in handy. "Please, Charles, just see what they have to say. Everybody in Topeka can't be wrong!"

After many discussions, Charles packed his suitcase with the manuscript neatly tucked inside and boarded a train for Chicago. But after meeting with two major publishers and being flatly rejected by both, Charles did exactly what his father-in-law had warned him against. Hat in hand, he arrived at the Advance Publishing Company and left with a contract. The company had agreed to publish two editions of *In His Steps:* a twenty-five-cent paperback edition and a clothbound book that would sell for one dollar.

For Charles, the first half of 1897 saw the realization of two precious dreams. On February 23, 1897, Charles and May's first (and only) child was born, a son whom they named Merriam. Growing up in a large and loving family, Charles had always wanted children, and he delighted in his blond, curly-headed son. Then in June 1897, both editions of *In His Steps* were released to the public.

From the outset the success of *In His Steps* was nothing short of astounding, and no one was perhaps more surprised than the two publishers who had rejected the manuscript. They, after all, had been the ones to tell Charles that "the strong religious character of the story. . .would make it a failure on the book market," he would recall decades later. However, within the first two years, Advance editions sold hundreds of thousands of copies, and the demand showed no sign of waning.

The Advance Publishing Company had its first runaway bestseller on its hands—and not a clue how to publish such a book. By 1899, the word was out: *In His Steps* was available to anyone for publication.

Under the spotlight of such national attention, the inadequacy of the small publisher's "standard copyright notice" soon became exposed. In truth, the Advance Publishing Company never applied for an official copyright for any of its published material. Anything published in its magazine, or for that matter, anything published at all by the company, was actually in the public domain. Charles was under the impression that the publisher had sent part of his manuscript to the copyright bureau in Washington, D.C., but even that effort would have proved inadequate. For an official copyright to be issued, the entire manuscript would have had to be received, which was not the case. A last-ditch effort by the Advance Publishing Company to secure an official copyright proved too little, too late. Other publishers were already issuing their own copies of *In His Steps,* and they would do so free and clear of any obligation to the initial publisher or the author.

Because of the oversight concerning the copyright, Charles would receive few royalty payments. As long as the Advance Publishing Company stayed in business (until the early 1900s), he received royalties of

10 percent, or around six thousand dollars, based on the number of copies they sold. He also received payments from a few other American publishers over the years, again adding up to a few thousand dollars. But unlike other authors of phenomenally successful books, Charles would not become wealthy because of *In His Steps*.

The copyright dilemma was not common knowledge to the general public, however. All too soon Charles was overwhelmed by letters from readers asking for financial help. "As hundreds of the letters insisted," he wrote years later, "the author who had profited to such an enormous extent and was rich ought to live up to the teachings of his book and share with the poor and unfortunate, with churches, and struggling authors, and cripples, and farmers in debt; lift mortgages, help pay off obligations incurred by persons who had lost the savings of a lifetime by bad investments, and especially help the missionary enterprises of the world to spread the Gospel."

One week the beleaguered pastor received more than nine hundred letters requesting donations. Charles could quote the standard request by heart: "Brother, take it to your heart, what would Jesus do? Surely you cannot imagine Him clinging to the wealth you have received from your book. He would surely share it with others who are in need. You cannot imagine him refusing my request. What would Jesus do?" He could not answer all these requests; he could only pray for those in such desperate situations. Most of all, he could and would not let himself become embittered.

The success of *In His Steps* continued at an almost unprecedented rate. In 1899, when the copyright was proved invalid, dozens of other publishers began publishing the book. In a few years, there were hundreds of different editions in the United States, with sales (by the year 1925) reaching eight million copies. In the early 1900s, foreign publishers seized the book as well, only contributing to the craze. In Great Britain alone, between twenty-five and thirty publishers decided to print the book, producing a wide variety of editions, from paper penny copies to illustrated holiday books. When Charles and May visited London, they had the pleasure of purchasing from a bookseller on the Strand a penny copy of *In His Steps* that bore the inscription, "This is the nine hundred and seventy-first thousandth copy." And that was the penny edition alone!

In Great Britain, *In His Steps* was not only one of the most popular books on the Strand, but it was also one of the most controversial topics spoken of from the pulpit. Sermons were preached supporting or denouncing whether church members should live their lives solely by asking what Jesus would do. Week after week, scholarly journals argued, according to Charles, "the theological soundness or unsoundness of the principles of the human conduct based on such an attempt to follow Jesus." A pamphlet entitled "The Rescue of

Loreen," written by Mrs. J. B. Horton, was issued in an attempt, again according to Charles, "to counteract the very dangerous influence of the original story."

Although Charles held no foreign language rights, when asked, he did request copies of newly translated editions. Of the many foreign editions, Charles estimated that his book had been translated into at least thirty-two languages, including (besides French, German, Italian, and Spanish) a dialect of Hindu, Arabic, Czech, Chinese, Greek, Portuguese, Telugu, Pasilaly, Russian, Armenian, Farsi, Gaelic, Esperanto, Turkish, Welsh, and Japanese.

Once again, the book proved to be a phenomenal success in large and small ways. A Japanese translator wrote to Charles, "I am looking out of my window and see two carpenters sawing on a timber; each one of them is holding a copy of your book in one hand and reading while he saws." In Persia, a translator used *In His Steps* as an English textbook when he taught in a Presbyterian mission. Likewise in Mexico, a missionary used the book as a regular part of the mission's curriculum. Charles was especially moved to read that during the Russian Revolution, a translator had been obliged to hide all copies of *In His Steps* in his cellar during the worst fighting. The power of Charles's message was also obvious in Turkey, where censors removed from the book all references to human freedom, brotherhood, the emancipation of women, and the cruelty of war.

129

Considering the number of publishers, both American and foreign, and the types of editions, there is no accurate estimate as to how many copies of the book have been sold worldwide, but it is surely in the tens of millions. However, just as he refused to succumb to regret or bitterness, Charles also did not want to dwell on any personal success. "But for all and any influence the book may have had," he wrote in 1925, "all the praise and wonder of it belongs to Him who alone among the sons of men is King of kings and Lord of lords." Nonetheless, he would be regarded from his fortieth year on as the author of one of the best-selling books of all time.

After the initial success of *In His Steps*, Charles began to mull over the dramatic possibilities of his book. Shortly before his father's death in 1912 (Charles's mother had died in 1905), Charles discussed the matter with the older Sheldon.

"Father, I'm not thinking of Broadway or any such grand stage," Charles said, gesturing with his hands. "Young people could perform such a play for church gatherings, for revivals, in support of prohibition, and so on. Do you believe it can be done?"

"Certainly the book has all the elements of a successful production, son. There's the very dramatic crisis with the tramp, not to mention the horrible scene at the Rectangle later on. And I wouldn't limit the play to young people, no sir. You would need mature actors to portray Henry Maxwell, Ed Norman, and some of the others, and then there's the grandmother of that heiress, what was her name?"

"Virginia Page, yes, you're right. But I'm not a dramatist, I have no experience writing plays."

"If that's your only problem, you haven't got any," his father replied with his usual calm. "Washburn College's just a stone's throw away, and you sure know a peck of people there. I bet some English professor is just waiting for you to call on him."

Washburn College was where Charles would find his dramatic collaborator, but not in the English department. Professor F. H. Lane, the head of the theater department, agreed to begin work at once on the project, but only if Charles would help him. Central Church became the site for the play's eventual debut, and many performances took place at the church during the course of Charles's ministry. His father would have chuckled had he lived to see the day when Charles himself agreed to portray Henry Maxwell in one of the church's productions.

While the play would later be turned into a musical as well as a radio drama, the most significant version was a lantern-slide production that premiered in 1900. Lantern slides, which were the precursors of photographic slides and movies, were hand-colored glass transparencies. The production was the brainchild of George Bond, a well-known lantern-slide maker in Chicago, who had professional actors pose for the slides and then put the results together in a show. Even Charles, who was skeptical at first of Bond's efforts, wrote the artist a letter in praise of the "photo play."

After Bond's show, it was inevitable that one day, when the technology was in place, Charles would negotiate the movie rights to *In His Steps*. But the problem of who owned the rights to the book soon became an issue. When the Advance Publishing Company, almost out of business at that point, claimed it owned the rights, Charles did not pursue the matter in court. Instead, he paid Advance five hundred dollars for the rights—which were considered practically worthless—and continued negotiations with the film company. Unfortunately, the film company was forced into bankruptcy before the project could be finalized.

In 1936 the Grand National Film Corporation, unbeknownst to Charles, issued a film with the surprising title *In His Steps*. But that was where the similarity between the book and film ended. The story of the movie concerned a young couple who defy their parents' wishes and elope to the country to begin a new life. Interviewed at the time, Charles had no difficulty conveying his outrage: "They [the film corporation] advertised it as being suggested by the story. It was a cheap melodrama that did not have a single character, scene, or lesson that is in the book. They even went so far as to advertise the film—'You have read the book, come and see the picture.' " Eventually,

Grand National Pictures, a successor to the Grand National Film Corporation, had the film renamed. Now billed as *Sins of the Children,* the film even came to a Topeka movie theater. Charles and May were never counted among the audience.

Charles would continue his writing career, eventually penning three sequels to *In His Steps*. While he was never to enjoy another outrageous success, he did receive general and critical acclaim for *The Everyday Bible,* a simplified retelling of the Bible that at one time was used in some Kansas public schools.

In 1900, though, flush from his recent acclaim, he launched into his next experiment, one that he had been wistfully considering for some time. Ed Norman, after all, was going to do it. . .why not Charles Sheldon?

nine

In March 1900, Charles made his dream to edit the Topeka *Daily Capital* a reality. But before he took that opportunity, he flipped through the pages of *In His Steps* one more time. He wanted to make sure he had the proper perspective; he needed to ask himself what Jesus would do if He were the editor. Turning to chapter 17, Charles found his answer in the words of Edward Norman:

1. *He [Jesus] would never allow a sentence or a picture in his paper that could be called bad or coarse or impure in any way.*
2. *He would probably conduct the political*

part of the paper from the standpoint of non-partisan patriotism, always looking upon all political questions in the light of their relation to the Kingdom of God, and advocating measures from the standpoint of their relation to the welfare of the people, always on the basis of 'What is right?' never on the basis of 'What is for the best interests of this or that party?' In other words, He would treat all political questions as He would treat every other subject, from the standpoint of the advancement of the Kingdom of God on earth.

3. *The end and aim of a daily paper conducted by Jesus would be to do the will of God. That is, His main purpose in carrying on a newspaper would not be to make money, or gain political influence; but His first and ruling purpose would be to so conduct His paper that it would be evident to all His subscribers that He was trying to seek first the Kingdom of God by means of His paper. This purpose would be as distinct and unquestioned as the purpose of a minister or a missionary or any unselfish martyr in Christian work anywhere.*

4. *All questionable advertisements would be impossible.*

5. *The relations of Jesus to the employees on*

the paper would be of the most loving character.

6. *As editor of a daily paper to-day, Jesus would give large space to the work of the Christian world. He would devote a page possibly to the facts of Reform, of sociological problems, of institutional church work and similar movements.*

7. *He would do all in His power in His paper to fight the saloon as an enemy of the human race and an unnecessary part of our civilization. He would do this regardless of public sentiment in the matter and, of course, always regardless of its effect upon His subscription list.*

8. *Jesus would not issue a Sunday edition.*

9. *He would print the news of the world that people ought to know. Among the things they do not need to know, and which would not be published, would be accounts of brutal prize fights, long accounts of crimes, scandals in private families, or any other human events which in any way would conflict with the first point mentioned in this outline.*

10. *. . .He would probably secure the best and strongest Christian men and women to co-operate with Him in the matter of contributions. . . .*

11. *Whatever the details of the paper might demand as the paper developed along its definite plan, the main principle that guided it would always be the establishment of the Kingdom of God in the world. This large general principle would necessarily shape all the detail.*

These dictates would be followed to the letter beginning in the weeks preceding Monday, March 13, 1900. As Charles sat in the offices of the *Daily Capital* two days before the start of the workweek—the first issue edited by him would come out on Tuesday, March 14—he rubbed his eyes and remembered his journey to this place. Like any journey, there had been and still were bumps in the road. Yet he felt more than ever that Jesus would bless his efforts, however humble, to honor Him in the pages of a newspaper.

For many years, there had been no indication that Charles would ever serve as editor of a Christian newspaper, even if only for one week. Of course Charles himself had planted the seed by presenting such a scenario in both *In His Steps* and in his first Sunday night serial novel, *Richard Bruce.* The subject had also come up in several sermons over the years, but to no avail. Clearly missing from real life was an heiress such as Virginia Page to finance the enterprise!

That changed during the summer of 1899. *In His Steps* had been a bestseller for two years, and it remained a hot topic of conversation, especially in Christian Endeavor circles. So popular was the concept of a congregation or an organization committing itself to doing as Jesus would, that the Christian Endeavor Society invited Charles to attend its national convention in Detroit as a featured speaker and guest.

Central Church had their own Endeavor chapter, one with which Charles had worked closely, especially after he had finished reading *In His Steps* to the congregation. Almost immediately, Central's chapter wanted to be among the first to "walk in His steps." Now Charles would be sharing his insights with thousands of Endeavor Society members at the convention—not to mention the more than four million members nationwide who would read his every word in the society's publications.

In his lectures, as he discussed the characters from his book, Charles found himself turning again to Ed Norman's plan for a Christian newspaper and how such a goal might be accomplished. His views weren't directed to Endeavor members only. During the convention, which was covered by the national media, Charles was interviewed regularly as the "famous author and pastor."

Anyone with a nose for news in Topeka couldn't help but notice the attention given a local pastor with rather unusual ideas, especially the idea of running his own newspaper. And anyone with a head for news in Topeka couldn't help but notice the marketability of such a notion.

As the new publisher of the Topeka *Daily Capital,* Frederick O. Popenoe was only slightly acquainted with Charles. Most of his information he derived from the glowing reports of the Endeavor convention in Detroit. He had recently settled in Topeka, having just purchased the paper in August, and he was eager to make a profit as quickly as possible. Popenoe envisioned that Charles Sheldon, the erstwhile editor, might be the stick of dynamite the *Daily Capital* needed to move from operating in the red to the black. Besides, Popenoe reasoned, religious publications were enormously popular, with subscription rates on the rise. Among the best known were the *Christian Herald,* the *Independent* (a Congregational weekly), the *Outlook,* and the *Ram's Horn*—and those were only the Protestant magazines. Numerous publications for Catholics, Jews, and Mormons also existed.

The publisher's invitation for Charles to join him at his home on November 3 seemed to the pastor like nothing more than an occasion to perform his civic duty. They, along with several other prominent Topekans, would be reviewing a military parade honoring the 20th Kansas Regiment. During the short-lived Spanish-American War of 1898, which was fought on more than one front, the fighting men of Kansas had brought honor to the state by their heroics in the Philippines, which had now become an American protectorate. More than five thousand Americans had died fighting in the islands.

Charles had become more comfortable in such social settings since his days in Vermont. He knew most of the men at the meeting—some from his weeks spent getting acquainted with the city—and they all had heard of him. The conversation was light and jovial with the usual backslapping and handshakes, and, of course, laudatory remarks for the marching soldiers and their feats in battle. The Spanish-American War had been, according to many political analysts, an excuse to flex the military muscle of the newest world power, to parade the newly united nation that was now greater than ever, its wounds healed sufficiently from the Civil War. Certainly no one was going to bring up religion, Charles thought to himself, remembering his own description of high society in many of his books, including *In His Steps*. And then he felt a tap on his shoulder.

"Mr. Popenoe," Charles said, a little startled. The slight, bespectacled publisher, his brown hair slicked down and combed in a severe center part, was standing almost uncomfortably close to him. Despite Popenoe's meek appearance, Charles was aware of his reputation as a formidable opponent in business dealings. But surely he didn't want to talk business with a preacher.

"Sheldon, I'd like a word with you when the other guests leave—if you have the time, that is." Used to barking orders, Popenoe wanted to tone down his request. Above all, he didn't want to sound too eager.

"Of course, that would be my pleasure," Charles answered graciously. As a pastor, he was often asked to consult privately with powerful men. Perhaps Popenoe had experienced a lapse of faith or was faced with a questionable business decision. In his mind Charles organized appropriate Scripture verses he could share with the publisher. Still, Popenoe didn't look troubled or distracted. Charles watched him as he carefully circulated around his living room, ever the attentive host. Well, whatever it was, Charles thought, he would find out soon enough.

When the last guest retrieved his hat and coat from the maid and departed, Popenoe motioned for Charles to join him in the sunroom. After asking whether he would care for more refreshment, the publisher cleared his throat.

"I've been reading your book lately, Sheldon," he began.

Charles knew "your book" referred to *In His Steps*, even though by now he had several titles published. Perhaps Popenoe thought that he could be Edward Norman, Charles thought suddenly and, he had to admit, with some envy. Here was a man with means who could produce a Christian newspaper! Gathering his wits, Charles knew he should say something in response, but he just smiled encouragingly, hoping the publisher would continue on his own.

"I just can't stop thinking about that newspaper editor, Norman, is it? He took such a powerful stand, despite criticism and bankruptcy and who knows what else. As one who lives and breathes printer's ink every day, his story touched me, I have to tell you."

"I'm glad to hear you say that, sir. That was my purpose in writing the book," Charles answered seriously, all the while looking keenly at the man seated next to him.

Looking down at his hands, Popenoe then raised his eyes to meet Charles's and grabbed the arm of his chair. "What I'm trying to say is, well, of course I've heard of your desire to serve as editor of a Christian newspaper, and I'd like to give you that opportunity. Here, in Topeka, at the *Daily Capital*, for one week. Anyone with your convictions deserves to have the chance to reach as many people as possible with good Christian news!"

Charles blinked his eyes and sat back in his chair. He was stunned, to say the least. Yes, he had campaigned for this moment, but he never thought it would happen like this.

"Well, Sheldon, what do you say? I can see I've caught you off-guard, and I'm sorry."

"No need for apologies, Mr. Popenoe, please. Yes, absolutely, I accept your offer! It's been my dream for many years, and the dream of others as well."

"I say the sooner, the better, Sheldon. In this business you can't sit on a good idea for too long or someone else will grab it. What do you say you take over the reins in March, four months from now? That should give me time to set the wheels in motion with all our personnel, advertisers, and so on."

"March? Yes, I suppose that will be fine. I'll have to advise my deacons and elders, but that should be no problem. Speaking of my position as pastor, and to avoid being accused of catering to outside interests, I don't believe I should receive any compensation for my work. Whatever I would have made should be donated to charity."

The publisher rubbed his chin and mumbled his assent.

"Mr. Popenoe, I must ask you this, though. You do intend to follow Edward Norman's suggestions, I mean, my suggestions for the newspaper? I can't serve as editor unless those rules are understood by everyone."

"Didn't I say that? Well, of course, Sheldon. That's the whole idea. The paper must be yours, based on *In His Steps*. You will have complete control of the newsroom. Only you will assign stories to reporters. I'm sure the entire staff will agree to work with you, but in any case, I'd appreciate it if you don't hire additional people."

Charles nodded his agreement, as if conceding a minor point. "And the advertisers? I can control which advertisements appear in the paper? That will mean no mention of liquor or tobacco—"

"Yes, yes, yes," Popenoe interrupted. "I'm not entirely sure how I'll work this out, but I'll see to it that all existing advertising contracts are suspended for one week. With the publicity this edition will generate, rest assured we won't have a dearth of advertisers! We will have to up subscription rates for the week, considering the cost of the mailings, but I'm sure you'll have no problem with that."

Again Charles nodded. "And the Sunday edition? You won't mind the loss of revenue, Mr. Popenoe? I can't agree to do this unless it's understood that there will be no Sunday paper and no newspaper employees will be working at any time on Sunday."

"Just as I said, Sheldon. Whatever you want short of ruining the plant or the offices or undermining the future of the paper is fine by me. You do as Norman did. To satisfy our subscribers, I do believe we should produce six editions in the week so that will likely mean two newspapers delivered on Saturday. You do realize you'll be working your brains out, don't you? Still want to do it? Do you still want to shake up the world?"

That question, however outrageous, was on Charles's mind, too. And he could tell that was what the publisher wanted, but undoubtedly for different reasons. Could Charles be salt and light in a world where mammon was king? Would he go on hiding his idea of a Christian newspaper under a basket, or would he expose it, as good deeds, to the light?

"Yes, sir. I can't begin to thank you, sir," Charles said humbly.

Brushing aside those words with a sweep of his

arm, Popenoe's face suddenly lit up with a wide grin. Charles found his expression a bit disconcerting. *Something about this proposition seems too good to be true,* Charles thought. *But I can't turn down what will likely be my only opportunity.*

As the publisher and the pastor shook hands energetically, sealing their verbal agreement, Popenoe exclaimed, "We'll call it the Sheldon Edition! Right at the top of the front page—on both sides of the banner headline!"

By January the groundwork had been laid, and soon all of Topeka was in on the secret. The January 23, 1900, edition of the *Daily Capital* proclaimed in its banner headline, "Rev. Charles M. Sheldon to Edit the Capital," and the entire front page was devoted to the story. Local clergy and politicians alike hailed the new edition and again praised Sheldon's work in Topeka and as an author of renown. Surely Edward Norman was alive and well and about to roll up his shirtsleeves and don his visor in the offices of the *Daily Capital*!

Soon subscriptions began coming in for the Sheldon Edition, and just as quickly, Popenoe began hiring extra help to take the orders. In fact, before the month of January was over, the *Capital* staff numbered more than forty, and six new mail carriers and office workers had been hired by the local post office.

But the wily publisher had a publicity plan in mind that would send subscription rates into the hundreds of thousands. To accomplish his plan, he hired two men, Herbert S. Houston and Auguste C. Babize, who had experience in advertising and publishing. Their first and most lucrative target would be the young men and women who were among Charles Sheldon's most vocal supporters: the Christian Endeavor Society.

A February issue of the Endeavor Society's publication contained a catchy advertisement, thanks to Houston and Babize. Club members who sold twenty-five-cent subscriptions to the Sheldon Edition of the *Daily Capital* would keep ten cents from each subscription sold for their own Endeavor chapter. The ad provided instructions on how and where to send lists of subscribers. Similar offers were made to Epworth League members and to YMCA and YWCA chapters across the country.

At the same time, newspapers around the country were enticed to take out subscriptions to the Sheldon Edition as a special bonus for new subscribers. Many of these newspapers were also encouraged to send their own reporters to Topeka for the week of March 13 to obtain firsthand coverage of this one-of-a-kind Christian newspaper. Frederick Popenoe took special pains not to discuss this latter arrangement with Charles. The new editor would not welcome the forty or so reporters who descended on the newsroom that week.

The results of Popenoe's campaign were astounding. The *Daily Capital* went from a daily circulation of less than 15,000 to more than 360,000 copies per day for the week of the Sheldon Edition. That brought to mind two more problems that would have to be solved well before March 13. How and where would the newspaper be printed, and how would the post office handle the mailing?

To ease the matter of printing and distribution, all issues of the Sheldon Edition would be confined to eight pages. Charles supported this move wholeheartedly but for a different reason. He felt it would be utterly impossible "for any one man to consider and pass on all the matter required to fill a larger paper." It would be difficult enough to find enough "original news" to fill eight pages.

Because the press at the *Daily Capital* could only print 120,000 copies of the eight-page paper a day, with men and women working around the clock, new printing sites were sought and found. Besides Topeka, the Christian newspaper would be printed at the offices of the *Chicago Journal;* the *Staats Zeitung,* a German language newspaper in New York City; and the *Westminster Gazette* in London. Every day during the week of March 13, a new set of printing matrices (from which to print the newspaper) would be sent from the *Daily Capital* plant. But it took time for the matrices to travel from Topeka to those sites. Consequently, the Sheldon Edition came out one day later in Chicago and two days later in New York. The London papers came out whenever the new matrices were received.

To handle the mailing, additional employees were hired, including a clerk to handle the influx of money orders that was flooding the post office on a daily basis. But someone was needed to oversee the special needs of the mailing operation. To fill that job, the Honorable Clyde Reed, the superintendent of the Railway Mail Service for Kansas, was enlisted. (Reed would later serve as governor of Kansas and as a U.S. senator.) Reed ingeniously created a post office out of two railway mail cars to carry the papers directly on their way. The distribution of the papers was set up in this way: All copies for subscribers east of Pittsburgh and in foreign countries were dispatched from New York; all copies for subscribers between the Alleghenies and the Missouri River were dispatched from Chicago; and all copies for subscribers west of the Missouri River to the Pacific Coast were dispatched from Topeka.

While Charles did not have a role in the more mundane facets of the newspaper, he was busy, as Popenoe had predicted. From the end of January to the debut of the paper, he spent half of every day just learning the newspaper business. He had had a taste of the work when he spent a week years earlier at the *Daily Capital,* but now his attitude had changed considerably. He was seriously determined to become an editor in more than name only.

He couldn't believe the sight that greeted him on his newly assigned desk every day. Stacked in haphazard piles that had once been neat were letters and cards from all over the country. Most folks had written to wish him well in his new endeavor, but others had tacked on a special postscript. These were fellow members of the clergy who hoped their compatriot in the ministry might see to including their articles in the Sheldon Edition. (He would ask clergy members, usually friends or well-known ministers, to contribute editorials to the newspaper, but these were men he asked, not those who wrote him.) At any rate, he tried to answer the letters as best he could, but as time went on he found he had other pressing concerns. It was time to decide which advertisements would appear in the paper.

From the first he found that he was rejecting nearly as many advertisements as those he deemed acceptable. *What if we don't fill all the advertising space?* he wondered anxiously. Charles didn't want to jeopardize the paper any more than necessary. *Mr. Popenoe did say I could run the paper the way Ed Norman would, though,* he reassured himself. That thought unspoken, he proceeded to review advertising copy during the last two weeks before the paper would be published.

Besides liquor and tobacco ads, Charles immediately rejected all ads for patent medicines that contained liquor. (Indeed, his staunch support for prohibition and his revulsion of saloons had surfaced in several of his novels and would form an important later chapter in his life.) He also opposed ads selling corsets because he felt they might be construed as too suggestive.

Automatically rejected as well were land and mining ads, the selling of stock by way of advertising, and those touting theatrical productions. Charles regarded the stock market as another excuse to gamble, and he would refuse coverage of its activities in the pages of his newspaper. Whenever possible, he supported ads by Topeka merchants—angering many Kansas City businesses—because he wanted the Christian edition of the *Daily Capital* to be a kind of hometown newspaper. He received numerous ads for books and magazines, but these he would only accept after he had personally reviewed the materials. Of course, any magazine that contained liquor ads was rejected immediately. To the copy of those advertisements that touted products Charles couldn't personally attest for, he inserted such words as alleged and supposed. He didn't advocate dishonesty from the pulpit, and he certainly wouldn't want to in his newspaper.

As Monday, March 13, drew near, Charles wrote down his own set of editorial rules. These were not printed for the staff. Rather, Charles communicated them to the employees at the beginning of the designated workweek and reinforced them as the days went by. Charles knew he had Mr. Popenoe's support, but some of these rules were, to say the least, a bit unusual. The first one was expected: There would be no drinking, smoking, or swearing in the *Daily Capital* offices or while any employee was on duty. All reporters, Charles felt strongly, must recognize that news is defined as "any event worth knowing or telling published in the right proportion to its importance." (To that statement, he noted in the margin, when telling the news, eschew slang for proper English.)

Like Edward Norman, Charles forbade lengthy coverage of "prize fights," as well as "scandals, crime, vice, or human depravity." The only sports news he deemed worthy of coverage was that of "healthy" amateur athletic events.

If crime news were reported, it first had to be "defined as evil" and accompanied by an editorial analysis of the reasons for the crime and how the crime could have been prevented. He had said many times that crime news should be reported in "the way the Bible always reports it"—in other words, to the point and without much embellishment. Charles had long felt that editorials should accompany articles rather than be relegated to an editorial page.

There would be no reporting of theatrical events or partisan political news. In a most unusual move, by-lines were to be included for all stories. In Charles's own words, this would be done "to ensure reliability, reward good reporting, and fix responsibility." This emphasis on responsibility extended to the procuring of interviews. Reporters were admonished by Charles to proceed with interviews only after obtaining the permission of the interviewee, and later, to receive the subject's written approval after the article had been written. Only then, following approval by Charles, would the article be printed.

The final editorial rule Charles would pass on to his attentive staff was obvious: In general, the standard of publishing should be what would Jesus do if He were publishing the *Daily Capital*. As he ventured boldly into the world of journalism, Charles would take comfort in the knowledge that he was never truly alone. He was walking in His steps.

Among the staff whom Charles warmly greeted on Monday, March 13, were Harold T. Chase, the associate editor; Dell Keizer, the business manager; J. Frank Jarrell, the news editor and head of the reporters; Robert Maxwell, foreman of the pressroom; and Jessie M. Garwood, the society and club reporter. (Jessie was engaged to be married to the newspaper's only Washington correspondent, John P. Fritts, who filed his reports via telegraph.) Developing a sense of rapport in the newsroom was important, but Charles was also anxious to get started on Tuesday's edition.

For the front page Charles wanted to print national or international news of importance, even though by the time such news reached Topeka it was old news that might have occurred weeks earlier. Still, he and Harold Chase perused the various stories from the wire reports. A wire report from the night before caught Charles's eye instantly. Why had he never read about this in the *Daily Capital*, or any other newspaper for that matter?

"There's a great famine going on in India and no paper in the United States has given it any prominence!" he exclaimed excitedly to Chase.

"Should it go on page one?" the editor asked tentatively.

"Absolutely! Let's make it the most important piece of world news," Charles shot back. That meant that the article would run in the left-hand column, the spot where the *Daily Capital* had always run a feature article. As Charles read the wire reports of the famine, he suddenly clapped his hands, causing Chase to jump in his seat.

"What is it, Reverend Sheldon?"

"This famine demands that we do something to help, Chase, that we ask our readers to help in some way. I'll have to work out the details, and of course, it wouldn't just be the *Daily Capital*. . . ." His voice trailed off as he sat thinking. "Yes, Chase, could you please write an article, or tell Frank to write one, asking for contributions to be sent to our office? We'll include it right on the first page, alongside the article about the famine."

Harold Chase looked slightly askance, but he would do as he was told. Besides, he liked Sheldon's refreshing way of looking at the news, and he liked the idea of offering tangible solutions to world problems.

Other than the story on the famine, which bore the headline "Starving India," the front page would feature articles on the recently ended Boer War, which

Sheldon bitterly opposed, a scathing commentary on the liquor industry as a catalyst of unemployment, and various testimonials praising prohibition. There was also a story on a Colorado YMCA that was trying to secure funds to build a sanitarium for tuberculosis patients, and another request for reader contributions. There would be no sensationalism, but as the pastor and editor had promised weeks earlier, there would be news that made readers think and search their souls.

While Charles inserted editorials immediately following certain news stories, he also maintained an editorial page on page two. There he printed his statement of purpose, a rehashing of the editorial rules he had established for his staff weeks earlier. Of special note was the masthead of the Sheldon Edition, which, instead of listing only the executives of the newspaper, gave the names of almost every person who worked at the *Daily Capital*, including the janitor and mailing room workers. Charles wanted the staff to be proud of their contributions.

Page 3 of the morning paper contained more international and national news, as well as items of interest in the state of Kansas. Sharing space with additional articles on the Boer War was news of a Methodist Church conference in Chanute, Kansas. A fire in a tenement in Newark, New Jersey, was described in detail, illustrating Charles's continuing compassion for the oppressed and needy. He was still, after all, active in Tennesseetown. Local news was printed on page 4, including stories of the continuing struggle for prohibition in Topeka.

The remaining pages of the Christian newspaper contained feature articles (page 5), a livestock market report, and classified and display advertising (pages 6 through 8). The largest ad was for *Christian Herald* magazine, a publication that was dear to Charles's heart.

Throughout the rest of the week, including Saturday morning's edition, Charles and Harold Chase debated over the most important news stories. By all accounts, it was a light news week with no war raging and no natural disaster occurring. Consequently, Charles, who had the final say, included stories on such topics as cigarette smoking (against); the status of kindergarten schools; a history of the Philippines; prison reform; Mormonism (against); tax dodgers; suffrage for women (in favor of); an appeal for cleaner humor; tenement house reform; the police department (an appeal for greater pay); dairy farming in Kansas (written by the Secretary of Agriculture of Kansas); Sunday school lessons from Topeka churches; and a protest of the massacre of Armenians in Turkey.

The new editor also put Jessie Garwood to work on a story he had long wanted to investigate. As the society and club reporter, the only position awarded to women journalists at the time, Garwood spent her days covering tea parties and luncheons, being sure to include who invited whom to what gathering. Perhaps sensing she was ready for a challenge, Charles gave her one: "Take an average day in Topeka and write about the wasted time and money spent in social frivolity on that day," being sure to include just how much money was "wasted."

After locating two receptions, three thimble parties, eight card parties, six dinners, five luncheons, two club dances, and a theatrical performance, Garwood reported the total cost of the day at $1716. An editorial, which followed the story and was obviously penned by Charles, implied that this money could have been better used to aid the relief efforts in India. Although the reaction from Topeka society was far from glowing, Charles stood his ground. "There are so many really important things going on in this world that the event of Mrs. Somebody invited other Mrs. Somebodies to a lunch or a dance. . .is so small that it does not deserve any place in a daily account of the doings of the sons and daughters of men," he wrote afterward.

The Saturday evening paper was, literally, a different story. No one who worked on this edition got much sleep, Charles included. In fact, throughout the week, he had been averaging three hours of sleep a night and had stayed in a downtown hotel instead of going all the way home. While he would stop in at 15th Street every morning for breakfast with May and their son, Merriam, his visits would be brief. The only other time Charles spent away from the newsroom was

Thursday night, when he presided over the prayer meeting at Central Church.

Even though he was physically exhausted, Charles was determined that no *Daily Capital* employee would work one second on Sunday. That meant that as soon as the Saturday morning papers went off the presses (around two in the morning on Saturday), the Saturday evening papers went on. The press and mailing work would stop just before midnight on Sunday. Obviously, the content for this evening paper had been prepared days ahead of time. Charles had determined that there would be no news in the journalistic sense in this paper. Instead, there would be reading appropriate for any family to consume on a Sunday. Almost ten years earlier, writing in *The Crucifixion of Philip Strong,* Charles had felt the Sunday paper in its bulky form was not appropriate reading material for the Sabbath:

> *Here is the reason why it seems to me*
> *Christ would, as I am doing now. . .avoid read-*
> *ing the Sunday paper, because it forces upon*
> *the thought of the community the very same*
> *things which have been crowding in upon it all*
> *the week, and in doing this necessarily distracts*
> *the man and makes the elevation of his spiritual*
> *nature exceedingly doubtful or difficult. I defy*
> *any preacher in this town to make much*
> *impression on the average man who has come*
> *to church saturated through and through with*

157

forty pages of Sunday newspaper. . . .

His views hadn't changed during the intervening decade. The headline of the lead story in the Saturday late edition of the *Daily Capital* that Charles edited revealed his intent: "The Bible: The Basis of Our Christian Civilization." The lead sentence was Daniel Webster's epitaph, written by the famous American and copied from his tomb at Marshfield, Massachusetts:

> *Lord, I believe. Help Thou mine unbelief. Philosophical argument, especially that drawn from the vastness of the universe in comparison with the apparent insignificance of this globe, has sometimes shaken my reason for the faith that is in me; but my heart has assured me that the Gospel of Jesus Christ must be a divine reality. The Sermon on the Mount cannot be a merely human production. This belief enters into the very depth of my conscience. The whole history of man proves it.*

Following this statement, Charles provided Jesus' Sermon on the Mount, printed in its entirety, from the Revised Version of the Bible. On the front page Charles also included a brief sermon (written by him) on the value of Sunday as a day of rest and worship.

To the subscribers of the *Daily Capital* he wrote an explanatory note: "There has been no Sunday work on this paper. The press and mailing work stopped before midnight of Saturday. The carriers were instructed to deliver their papers in time to reach home themselves before Sunday. There will be no papers sold or delivered on Sunday with the approval of the editor. May God bless the use of the press of the world to the glory of His kingdom on earth."

The rest of the Saturday evening paper—there were still eight pages—contained mostly Bible teaching. What does the Bible have to say about usury, the Sabbath, money and riches, marriage, the evil of drink, war, the future, and love? Charles provided biblical answers, as well as a summary of the Bible in history, furnished by the American Bible Society. Another advertisement for *Christian Herald* featured its "red letter" New Testament.

At week's end Charles had fulfilled his obligation to Frederick Popenoe and to the paper's wide readership. Whether or not he was successful was a matter open to debate.

Conspicuously missing from the list of names on the masthead on page 2 of the Sheldon Edition was that of Frederick O. Popenoe, publisher. At the time Charles would offer no explanation. Years later, writing about the experience, he expressed his outrage at the presence of the forty reporters who were encouraged to come to Topeka, indirectly at least, by Popenoe. "I did not welcome [the reporters]," wrote Charles, "and shall always believe that their presence was undesirable and unfair." According to Charles, these newshounds constantly demanded interviews, and each one wanted to present a different angle to their hometown papers "that contained more imagination and less fact than the most brilliant writer of fiction ever dreamed." In short, Charles felt that these newsmen, invited without his permission by the publisher, did not give him a fair chance to put out the kind of final product he wanted.

The final product was indeed subject to criticism. While most of the country's newspapers reported on the Sheldon Edition during the week, the general consensus in the general press was that the paper was "deadly dull" and "hopelessly boring." The clergy, by and large, supported Charles's efforts, especially those who shared his vehement stands on prohibition and war. Still, there were those clergy, and they were a vocal minority, who objected to the thought of Jesus Himself supposedly taking over a daily paper. They invariably attached the words blasphemous, sacrilegious, and irreverent to their critiques.

For the most part, Charles stayed out of the fray. He saved most of his comments, which he wrote years later, for those clergy who cried blasphemy. "The entire concept of Christianity to my mind is entirely stripped of its tremendous meaning if we do not think of Jesus as the most vitally interested Being that ever lived, in the common everyday doings of humanity," he wrote. "Hundreds of ministers in these press notices said that Jesus would never descend to anything except preaching. They seem to forget that the greater part of His life was passed in a carpenter's shop, and that the tables and benches and common wooden things in many a home of Nazareth were doubtless made by His hands. . . . We have no such thing as Christianity unless we have a definition of it in terms of abundant life, as wide as man's activity, and as sacred as the everyday toil of the hands of Him Who was nailed on a cross. . . two thousand years ago."

Such criticism notwithstanding, Charles Sheldon's Christian newspaper was successful on several levels. A tidy profit of tens of thousands of dollars was gained from the week's newspapers, though figures vary as to how much. Charles himself, who refused to accept a salary, was given five thousand dollars in appreciation of his work. He did not keep it. Instead, he donated part of it to the famine relief fund and part to building a public water fountain in Topeka.

The most widely publicized success was the newspaper's efforts to provide relief for people suffering through the famine in India. Between 1900, when Sheldon issued the call for funds, until 1904, readers of the *Daily Capital* sent fifty thousand dollars to India. As a direct result of Sheldon's appeal, a train load of Kansas corn was sent by local farmers first to New York and then, via chartered ship, to Bombay, India. The *Christian Herald* was instrumental in assisting Charles in this endeavor and in soliciting funds for the relief effort as well.

Months later Charles received heartwarming letters from missionaries in India telling of hundreds and perhaps thousands of cases where this Kansas corn had literally saved lives. "Sometimes when people have asked me if the paper were not a failure, as the press reports for the most part said it was," Charles would say, "I have replied that if it accomplished nothing more than saving several thousand children from starvation I would always feel as if the paper was a success, if it did nothing else."

There were smaller measures of success, too. Charles's emphasis on the responsibility of reporters, his adamant stands for truth in advertising, and his restraint in how he reported sensational news stories were praised by many. Of note was his treatment of the suicide of a young man who had been fired by the *Daily Capital* on the Saturday before the start of the Sheldon Edition. The young man, who died over the weekend from an overdose of morphine, happened to be the son of a former U.S. senator from Kansas and current resident of Topeka. The first thing Charles's reporters wanted to do was to rush to the family's home, but the new editor would have none of it. Instead, Charles printed a single paragraph on one of the inside pages giving only the essential facts of the death and offering sympathy to the senator and his wife. "I see nothing to be gained by relating the ghastly details of human frailty and sin," wrote Charles.

Years later he would be asked to serve as religion editor of various daily papers across the country. Charles turned down all offers. He had accomplished Edward Norman's goals, he had done as he thought Jesus might have, and in the process he had been battered in a storm of controversy and criticism. He would go back to the familiar pulpit of Central Church, but only until another cause soared in his soul and pricked again his sense of outrage.

ten

At the January 25, 1912, annual meeting of Central Church, Charles Monroe Sheldon resigned as minister, effective the following June. Widespread dismay greeted his decision: He had been the shepherd of an ever-growing flock for almost twenty-four vigorous, passionate years. But his parishioners also realized, or at least most did, that only a cause dear to his heart and soul would lead him elsewhere.

Before he left the pulpit he would be given a new title, "Minister-at-large." That would suit him in his new role. *It implies I'm an ambassador of sorts, which is what I will be, and that I have a message to share, which I do,* he thought. Moreover, he was pleased with the congregation's choice of his successor. Roy Guild, executive secretary of the Men and Religion Forward Movement, had spent his childhood years in Topeka. For the next three years Central Church would be in able hands.

Charles was leaving to lend his full-time support to the cause of prohibition, an issue he had long supported. Twenty years earlier he had walked down Kansas Avenue in Topeka and felt his blood boil at the sight of alcohol abuse. A few years later, he had penned his anguish and frustration over the saloon in his Sunday evening novels, among them *The Crucifixion of Philip Strong*:

> *What [Philip Strong] saw after a dozen visits to as many different groggeries added fuel to the flame of indignation that burned already hot in him. The sight of the vast army of men turning into beasts in these dens created in him a loathing and a hatred of the whole iniquitous institution that language failed to express. He wondered with unspeakable astonishment in his soul that a civilized community in the nineteenth century would tolerate for one moment the public sale of an article that led, on the confession of society itself, to countless crimes against the law of the land and of God.*

When he put pen to paper and created *In His Steps*, Charles's position had shifted slightly. Still the passionate advocate, he would place the onus of responsibility to rid the nation of saloons and the like on the Christian community, as illustrated by the following excerpt from the book when the hapless Loreen is killed by a bottle of liquor in the infamous Rectangle:

And yet this is only one woman out of thousands killed by this drink evil. Crowd back, now, ye sinful men and women in this filthy street! Let this august dead form be borne through your stupefied, sobered ranks! She was one of your own children. The Rectangle had stamped the image of the beast on her. Thank Him who died for sinners that the other image of a new soul now shines out of her pale clay. Crowd back! Give them room! Let her pass reverently, followed and surrounded by the weeping, awestruck company of Christians. Ye killed her, ye drunken murderers! And yet—and yet— O Christian America, who killed this woman? Stand back! Silence, there! A woman has been killed. Who? Loreen. Child of the streets. Poor, drunken, vile sinner. O Lord God, how long, how long? Yes. The saloon killed her; that is, the Christians of America, who license the saloon. And the Judgment Day only shall declare who was the murderer of Loreen.

In 1892 and in 1896, writing those words, Charles had acted on his feelings, and he was not about to stop now. Not when there was a chance that he could persuade hundreds and maybe thousands of people how much better off they'd be if the entire United States could someday be a dry country. To him, the saloon—or the speakeasy or the "drugstore," as it was also called—was one of the worst evils affecting society. It was time for history to be written.

Alcohol abuse in eighteenth-century Europe, following the improvement of distillation technology, came to be commonplace in the American colonies as well. By the early 1800s, the average American was consuming almost ten gallons of pure alcohol per year, a shocking fact that finally spurred religious and political leaders to take some action.

In 1851 Maine became the first state to pass a prohibition law that prohibited the manufacture and sale of alcohol "not intended for medicinal or mechanical purposes." Other states quickly followed suit, and by 1855, thirteen of the thirty-one states—Kansas was not among them—had such laws on their books. Not coincidentally, the rate of alcohol consumption dropped to less than three gallons per person.

Such progress in the prohibition movement would be halted, however, with the start of the Civil War and all but forgotten in the devastating aftermath of that conflict. By 1870, an estimated one hundred thousand saloons were thriving in the United States.

Once again the prohibition troops were organized, led at first by thousands of women who marched, prayed, and sang in the "Women's War" of 1873. They wanted saloons to close their doors for business. The results were decidedly mixed, but promising signs could be seen in Kansas: Effective May 1, 1881, the first prohibition amendment in that state became law, prohibiting the manufacture and sale of intoxicating beverages, except for medicinal purposes.

In theory, according to the local press, Kansas's law meant "liquor is kept out of the general consciousness, and particularly out of the consciousness of the young." But in truth, while Kansas had succeeded in abolishing the saloon, it had certainly not stopped the flow of alcohol. Bootlegging, or the illicit retail distribution of liquor, was enjoying a brisk business, as was the sale of supposedly dry beverages such as cider, which were now billed as "fortified" to disguise their alcohol content.

Sales were flourishing in Topeka, where by some counts, forty establishments known as "open saloons" were considered legitimate by law. To Charles they were known as "drugstores." The average citizen could walk into any one of twenty-five drugstores on Kansas Avenue alone, swear to a particular ailment (by signing his name to the druggist's "permit"), and walk out of the store with several bottles of beer or whiskey. These permits, which were filed in the city's probate court, were open to inspection by any private citizen, but Charles surmised few had taken advantage of that right.

Charles himself examined the records and discovered a shocking truth: Under the cloak of medicinal need, prominent members of Topeka society, alongside less influential citizens, were consuming alcohol freely. One man astounded Charles with his gall. For one month he had purchased alcohol every day, and recorded a different disease for every purchase, including the dubious notation of "water on the stomach" for the final day of the month! "The condition lay heavy on my soul, for no one seemed to care," Charles wrote years later.

That particular day in 1892 as Charles stood observing Topekans flagrantly flaunting the law, he ran into a deacon of Central Church. A. G. Carruth was a man whom Charles respected greatly, so much so that the pastor claimed the deacon's middle initial could stand for "Gospel."

"Have you noticed the situation here, brother?" Charles asked the deacon. "Can we just stand by and watch as families are destroyed by drink?"

"I'm as distraught as you, Reverend Sheldon. The situation has indeed become unbearable," he answered.

Charles thought for a brief moment before hatching his plan. He wasn't considering the cost to himself or his ministry. He was hoping A. G. would want to get as involved as he. When he asked the deacon for

169

support, the answer was immediate.

"When do we start?"

"Right now," answered the minister with a new mission.

The two men headed off for the nearest drugstore. Charles's plan was simply to purchase liquor without signing any permit, with Carruth as a witness, and take the "evidence" to the county attorney. However, when the moment came for the liquor bottles to be handed to Charles by the druggist, Carruth, who was standing behind Charles, didn't actually see the exchange. He did witness the money changing hands, but that was all.

After a long and bitter legal contest waged by the lawyer representing the drugstore, the case was eventually thrown out of court. Charles was nonetheless filled with admiration for his deacon. Even though the county attorney had advised A. G. Carruth to say that he saw the transaction, the deacon would not lie.

This defeat would not deter the minister and deacon from their mission, however. A few days later they were back on the street, securing more evidence from numerous drugstores and "joints" in Topeka. But now that they had begun to fight the good fight against liquor, the two became marked men for the liquor merchants. While Charles escaped harm, A. G. suffered a broken leg when unknown assailants attacked him, an injury that laid him up for months. In addition, both men received anonymous hate letters, advising them to desist from their actions.

170

"Don't let up for a minute, Charles," A.G. pleaded when the minister came for one of his frequent visits. "I have no regrets, despite what happened. But it's up to you now. All we need are a few convictions before folks realize we mean business."

In the months that followed, justice was finally served—for the most part. After one druggist was found guilty of selling liquor to Charles, he appealed his case to the Democratic governor of the state and received a full pardon. The cases against other druggists were a different story. Over twenty convictions were made, and soon the county jail was filled to capacity.

Even as the anonymous hate letters continued, Charles found himself filled with compassion for the jailed men and for their families. Now that their source of income had been cut off, their families were often left destitute. They needed help, and Charles believed the church should provide that assistance. While Central Church's Ladies' Aid Society visited the families of the jailed men, Charles was a regular visitor to the county prison. The ladies paid grocery bills and the rent and provided medical care; Charles brought books and newspapers to the jail and invited the men and their families to come to church when they were able. He even lent his money to them.

Charles also succeeded in closing what he called one of the worst joints in Topeka, located in Tennesseetown. When the owner heard of his impending arrest, he paid a personal visit to the pastor to make an unusual appeal.

"How much do you want for your kindergarten?" he growled at Charles.

Looking at the burly man, Charles didn't know what to make of the comment. He knew that two of the man's children attended the Tennesseetown kindergarten, but did that merit a personal visit?

"I'm not sure I understand what you're saying, sir," Charles answered calmly.

Pulling out a roll of bills from his pocket, the man said gruffly, "Look, I can't waste any more time. Here's two hundred if you will call the police off my place."

Even though the kindergarten was going through a particularly bad time financially, and Charles had no idea where he would find the funds to pay the next month's bills, he could not accept money earned from the sale of liquor for the school. He did plead with the man to clean up his place of business for the sake of his children, since the school was indeed trying to turn them into upstanding citizens, but Charles failed to move the man. That night, the police closed down the joint, sending a message to similar businesses in Tennesseetown. They soon faded away as well.

As Charles became more involved in the prohibition movement, he crossed the paths of other equally dedicated crusaders, chief among them Carry A. Nation. Born in Missouri, Carry settled in 1890 in

Medicine Lodge, Kansas, where her second husband, a minister, had been called to a church. The evils of drink were never far from her thoughts—her first husband's death was attributed to alcohol—and in Kansas she saw plenty to raise her ire. But unlike Charles, who had taken a nonviolent approach to change, the almost six-foot-tall Carry flexed her muscles and grabbed her hatchet.

After asking God to save Kansas, on June 1, 1900, in the small town of Kiowa, Carry Nation smashed the windows of the first of many "open" saloons. Although Carry was often arrested for breaking the law, Charles held her in high esteem, inviting her on more than one occasion to speak at Central Church. According to Charles, after Carry Nation, law enforcement became not the exception but the rule in dealing with prohibition violators.

Carry Nation's crusade against saloons would end just as Charles's most important years as a prohibitionist were about to begin. Her days of "hatchetation" over, she would die penniless and alone on June 9, 1911. On her tombstone the formidable advocate had requested this epitaph: "She Hath Done What She Could." Charles Sheldon, however, knew that he still had work to do.

Charles had resigned from Central Church so that he could preach prohibition, and the first item on his agenda was a trip almost around the world, sponsored by the Young Men's Christian Association. Traveling with May and their young son, Merriam, Charles preached in Hawaii (the islands of Oahu and Maui), Australia (Sydney and Melbourne), and New Zealand (from Wellington to Christchurch and many stops in between).

From a political standpoint, his trip couldn't have been planned at a worse time. He visited Australia at the very moment Great Britain entered World War I. The Aussies, in particular, were more interested in "God Save the Queen" than in saving themselves from the evils of alcohol. Suspicious of all foreigners, Australian policemen even confiscated Merriam Sheldon's camera as he snapped photos of Sydney Harbor, only to return it later, minus the film. The Great War had begun, and Charles held out little hope for worldwide prohibition until the last shots were fired.

In early September 1914, Charles boarded a train from Victoria, British Columbia, bound for Seattle. He was looking forward to being back in the United States, and he was excited at the prospect of doing some work that might be appreciated, given that his international campaign for prohibition hadn't gone quite the way he planned.

Once in Seattle, after seeing May and Merriam off on another train going home to Topeka, Charles went to the designated meeting place for members of the newly formed "Flying Squadron." For the next eight months or so, he would be a member of one of three teams that would crisscross the entire country, spreading the message of national prohibition through both speeches and songs. He was almost sixty years old, but he had never felt more alive or invigorated.

Charles felt honored to be chosen, and proud of the two men who had had the foresight to conceive of such a mission. The Flying Squadron—named for the speed of the mission, not the mode of transportation—was the brainchild of Governor J. Frank Hanly of Indiana, who would later be a Prohibition Party candidate for president, and Oliver Wayne Stewart of Illinois. Hanly and Stewart had already addressed large rallies in several states and had been overwhelmed by the response. There was a need for a contemporary, entertaining program that also preached national prohibition. Besides, the only way to make prohibition part of the U.S. Constitution was to take the message to the people and make it a message they would turn out in droves to hear. The two men selected musicians, ministers, and other well-known public speakers to make up the three teams. These prohibition programs would be lively, humorous, and thought provoking—entirely different from anything tried before.

The national campaign of the Flying Squadron began officially on September 30, 1914, in Peoria, Illinois, dubbed by Charles as "the biggest whiskey center" in the country. "The first group of speakers, singers, and musicians had two meetings, one in the afternoon, and one in the evening, took up a free will offering to defray the expenses of the Squadron, and moved on the next morning to Galesburg, Illinois," Charles recorded some years later. "The second group moved into Peoria and held the same meetings there while the first group was in Galesburg, and when they moved on to Galesburg, the third group started their meetings in Peoria as the first group went on to Kansas City, Missouri."

So the pattern was established. Three different teams offering three entirely different programs over the course of three successive days would entertain audiences in each city on the Squadron's itinerary. Geographically speaking, it was a grueling schedule. October found the Squadron in Illinois, Missouri, Kansas, Oklahoma, Texas, Arizona, California, Nevada, and Washington; during the month of November the teams went in and out of fourteen states.

Continuing at that pace exacted a personal toll on the team members, Charles included. "The erratic train schedule of the Squadron made anything like regular physical habits absolutely impossible," he stated. "The evening meetings never closed before nine-thirty; oftener if would be ten o'clock before we were back at the hotel to pack up, count the offering, or if impossible to pour it into a suitcase and make a hurry run to the train for the night ride to the next town. Meals were eaten at any hour. . . . We ate at three and four o'clock A.M. in Greek restaurants. We broke every rule of diet and sleep and exercise and every rule of rest and recreation. . . . All of us lived at a high and abnormal pitch."

Although some money had been raised by Hanly and Stewart to launch the Squadron, free-will offerings, as mentioned by Charles, were collected during each program to pay for the next day's rail travel and for the living expenses of that particular team. No salaries were guaranteed to any musician or speaker; working for the cause itself would be all the reward any team member would expect to receive. (When all bills were paid at the end of the tour, however, each member did receive less than one hundred dollars apiece.)

Charles enjoyed his particular role at the end of the day—that of "Holy Roller"! Late at night, the day's offering spread out on his hotel bed, Charles was responsible for counting the coins and rolling them into brown paper wrappers. Never before had he handled so much money, and never before had he been so touched by sentiments often expressed with the gifts. Written on the "money envelopes" were messages that Charles loved sharing with the rest of the team: "With a prayer"; "Cash. Keep it going"; "A saved booze fighter"; "All right, Governor"; "God help you fight the traffic for the sake of my boys"; "I wish it were $10,000"; "God speed the work"; and "Five dollars in memory of Lincoln's Birthday, 1915."

Charles could only imagine the extensive planning that had gone into making the Squadron a reality.

Railroad timetables had to be scoured so that the teams would arrive one after the other. Churches had to be contacted in the various cities to ensure their cooperation (and hospitality). Publicity had to be generated via advertisements in newspapers and posters hung in public places.

The statistics of such a venture were staggering. Over the course of eight months—Saturdays and Sundays included but with one week off for Christmas—the three teams stopped in 255 cities in 235 days (sometimes visiting two cities in one day), without missing a single date on their itineraries. From Peoria in September to their final program in Atlantic City, New Jersey, on June 6, 1915, the members of the Flying Squadron traveled some sixty-five thousand miles and entertained a collective audience of 1.5 million people.

If the Flying Squadron were a grand notion, it could only be traced to the statement of purpose issued by Governor Hanly before the campaign began:

> *Our field is the United States; Our dream a Saloonless Land, a Stainless Flag, a Sober People; To be attained through an enlightened, an aroused, and a crystallized public opinion. We are not officially connected with any other existing temperance organization. We are the friends of all; the enemies of none. We war only against the Liquor Traffic. The campaign in which we are engaged has, we believe, no*

parallel in the history of any movement. When completed it will be without precedent. While we go to help any local fight that may be on, or any state contest that may be waging, ours is the National struggle. We battle for the nation. The event is in the hand of God.

The "battle for the nation" would be a glorious triumph for those who served in the Flying Squadron. By 1916, twenty-three of the then forty-eight states had adopted antisaloon laws. Moreover, in the national elections that year, those members who were returned to the U.S. Congress were overwhelmingly in favor of prohibition. On December 22, 1917, Congress submitted to the states the 18th Amendment to the Constitution, an amendment that prohibited "the manufacture, sale, or transportation of intoxicating liquors." The 18th Amendment was ratified by January 1919.

By many accounts, the Flying Squadron, a campaign like no other, was influential in bringing about a law without precedent.

Following the arduous campaign of the Squadron, Charles returned to his home in Topeka. He had missed his wife and son, and he soon realized how much he'd missed his beloved Central Church congregation. When Roy Guild resigned in March 1915 to pursue another ministry, the congregation voted to reinstate their former pastor when he returned from his prohibition commitments. As soon as Charles had a chance to catch his breath, he discovered he wanted very much to return to pastoral work and he accepted the offer with pleasure. For the next four and a half years he would devote himself to preaching, writing novels to be read on Sunday nights, and various outreach projects in the community. And for one three-month period—for which he was granted a leave of absence—he would travel to England.

In 1917, in the final months of the Great War, Charles would make another plea for prohibition. He had taken to heart British Prime Minister David Lloyd George's statement, "We are fighting Germany, Austria, and drink; and as far as I can see, the greatest of these three deadly foes is drink." This would actually be Charles's third trip to England in support of prohibition—the other two made in 1900 and 1908—and he was well acquainted with the country and well loved by its people. Because of the huge publishing success of *In His Steps* in Great Britain, Charles Sheldon could command large audiences whenever—and on whatever subject—he spoke.

Under the auspices of the National Temperance Foundation of Great Britain, Charles traveled the countryside, visiting seventy-five towns in two months. On his previous trips he had been shocked to see so many saloons and so much public drunkenness. In the early war years, the country rationed food but not liquor. During his third visit, however, as he wrote years later,

"I saw American and Canadian and Australian boys drunk on the streets, and at Plymouth the crews of three of our battle ships lay drunk in the streets for nearly a week. . . ." Charles's pleas to those who sold liquor to stop "debauching the soldiers and sailors of the Allies" fell on deaf ears. In pubs all over England and Scotland, Charles observed printed notices in the windows that read, "Men in uniform served here to whiskey and brandy. Others to beer only."

Upon his departure for home in January 1918, Charles carried with him a letter from Sir George Hunter, a leader of the National Prohibition Movement in Great Britain and the builder of such well-known vessels as the *Mauretania* and *Lusitania*. The letter, which was addressed to U.S. President Woodrow Wilson, pleaded for some action to be taken to protect American soldiers from the evils of drink. Charles would deliver the letter to the White House, and though he would not meet with the president, he did get an audience with Herbert Hoover, then the designated U.S. food administrator, responsible for feeding the Allied Armies. The dedicated prohibitionist wasted no time in baring his soul to Mr. Hoover, who gave him every assurance that something would be done if possible.

"It is a fact that much of our grain to Great Britain was afterwards sent in the form of flour instead of grain," Charles wrote later. Aside from that, he held out little hope that Great Britain would one day be a dry country.

As he celebrated his sixty-first birthday in Topeka, his suitcase put away in the attic for the time being, Charles knew his days of active ministry were waning. Like Carry Nation and like his Uncle Joe on the frontier, he had done what he could to stem the flow of liquor. But had he done enough for his adopted home on the prairie? What indeed would be his legacy—and when was it time to say good-bye?

eleven

For thirty years, give or take his three-year hiatus and shorter leaves of absence, Charles Sheldon had remained devoted to Central Church and to the people of Topeka, Kansas. There had been many offers of employment elsewhere—enticing, lucrative offers that might have swayed many a poorly compensated pastor—but not one so in love with the prairie and prairie folks.

He said once that in Kansas he could "see a lot of scenery in the sky." That wide-open feeling, the sense that one can reach for the stars, was part of his job description at Central Church. Charles felt sincerely that no minister ever enjoyed as great a sense of independence as he. "I never knew a single moment of fear or question in my mind as to the liberty I had to do and say what I wanted to," he wrote. "I knew always that the strong and individual men in the parish often differed from me in matters theological and political, and they were not slow in telling me so. But when it came to acting on my own initiative in the pulpit or in public I knew without their telling me, that the field was open without the slightest hint of opposition or even advice unless I asked for it." Put another way, there was, as he would aptly describe, "no suspicious or restricted circle" about his preaching and his "parish ministrations."

Charles prized that air of freedom, which he likened to the freshness of the prairie breezes "that start somewhere in the Rocky Mountains and do not stop until they hit the Alleghenies, and begin to get discouraged only about the time they reach the New York Palisades." Indeed, without that sense of independence, Charles's pastorate might have been at best undistinguished—and at worst, short-lived.

There were his many weeks spent "getting acquainted" with the city of Topeka, followed by his time-consuming but extremely satisfying years spent transforming attitudes and establishing reforms in Tennesseetown. There were his trips to Chicago and his speaking engagements that stemmed from the publishing of *In His Steps*. There were the months spent preparing for the Sheldon Edition of the Topeka *Daily*

Capital. And prior to his temporary resignation from the church, there was the summer of 1910, when he was appointed by then Mayor R. S. Cofran to a brief term as police commissioner of Topeka.

His appointment came after he expressed his not inconsiderable opinions—in a Sunday sermon—on the "right way to police a city." He also felt that the entire police system of the time was, in a word, wrong. Charles espoused a missionary police force of men and women, one that would be well equipped to "work miracles of redemption among the most depraved and degraded peoples." These compassionate police officers would, like the editor of a Christian newspaper, look for the causes of the crime instead of focusing on the symptoms. They would also, like missionaries, get to know everyone under their care (or their beat) and offer help in other areas, such as health and physical fitness, to better equip their people to deal with the rigors of life.

One of Commissioner Sheldon's first acts was to appoint the first policewoman in Topeka, Miss Eva Corning. Although she experienced ridicule and distrust, according to Charles, her reports sent back to the department "were filled with wise suggestions." Unfortunately, her employment was cut short after Charles's term expired. Despite his good intentions, the Topeka force largely ignored his other suggestions for reform.

Throughout his career in Topeka, Charles's messages and cries for reform seemed to touch the young more than the old. They, more than their parents and grandparents, followed him back to Central Church after working side by side with him during the week. They were the first to raise funds for the kindergarten in Tennesseetown and then to volunteer to work in the school and library. They were the first to want to mirror the fictional Henry Maxwell's congregation of *In His Steps,* to live as Jesus would have them. They also wanted to join Topeka's police force, spurred on by their desire to be missionaries. And when Charles issued the cry from the pulpit for the fair treatment of Jews, Catholics, and followers of other religions as well as equal rights for women, including full equality in the workplace, they rallied wildly around him. That they joined Central Church in large numbers was no surprise.

When the church moved in 1889 from its humble meeting place above the meat market to its permanent building, it had about one hundred members. By 1914, more than one thousand people were members, most under the age of forty. This represented about fifty new members per year.

Still, Charles would have been the first to say that he did not build Central Church alone. It was, as he said, a "twofold thing, composed of pulpit and pew." Typical of the man, Charles admitted that he could not preach effectively to the people in his church on a Sunday unless he could say he knew and loved them on a Monday. "I always had a conviction that somehow before another Sunday came around," he once said, "I would earn my salary by helping someone during the week that I had missed when I tried to preach to him."

"Helping someone" included making pastoral visits, occasionally surprising a parishioner by showing up on his doorstep on his birthday with a special gift; establishing a church emergency fund to provide loans for those members in need; and purchasing a cemetery plot at Topeka's Mount Hope Cemetery where Central Church members who could not afford a burial plot would be buried without charge. He did not regard himself as an evangelist, at least not in the style of his contemporaries Dwight Moody and Billy Sunday, noting that "very few churches are built up by evangelistic efforts made to reach outsiders." Rather, he felt that "all ministers ought to be able to evangelize their own people by regular methods of preaching and teaching."

When more and more young people in Topeka responded to his messages—and his actions during the week—they started coming to Sunday school at Central Church. Charles responded to their increased attendance by devoting himself to them. He spent time every week crafting Sunday sermons for children, as well as being available to them for spiritual counseling. It was not unusual for a seven year old to be received into full church membership, provided the child's parents agreed with the decision. According to their pastor, these children understood "what the Christian life meant, and what church membership meant, not with an adult mind but with a child's mind, and there were very few lapses

187

as they grew up into the church life." As the years of his ministry passed, Charles would witness many of these Sunday school attendees grow up to become missionaries.

In 1919, at the age of sixty-two, Charles Sheldon resigned for good from Central Congregational Church. The previous year had seen him in and out of the hospital, first for an operation and then for a cracked rib after taking a fall on the ice. Physically, he simply could not continue to serve at the only pace he deemed acceptable—a most vigorous one. His retirement would be bemoaned and his ministry celebrated for years to come.

For the past twenty years or so he had been besieged with correspondence, mostly concerning *In His Steps*. Now that he had officially retired, however, he began to hear more from seminary students and clergymen. Undoubtedly, they surmised, the grand old man, dubbed "Saint Charles" or "Charles the Good" by some, had more time on his hands to look back and reflect on his unusual and illustrious career. What were the tenets of his ministry? What, indeed, could he pass on to those who had accepted the call to devote their lives to serving Jesus Christ? It was his pleasure to respond. To Charles Sheldon, there was no greater calling.

November 10, 1919

Dear Friend in the Service of Jesus Christ,
My creed after more than thirty years in

188

the ministry is the same as it was after I graduated from Andover Theological Seminary in 1886. The only creed that has seemed to me to be workable and practical is the creed of Jesus—Love to God and Man. The attempt to carry out that creed in everyday life has kept me so busy that I have not been interested in the theological discussions over the person of Christ, the future of the heathen, or the value of denominationalism. All I feel certain about is that God breathed into man the breath of life and man became a living soul.

I would not dare to call myself a minister or a preacher if I had not at the beginning of my pastorate settled some things clearly in my mind that I am able to put down as my concrete program of faith and practice in the ministry, all of it based on the one great fundamental of love to God and man. These pledges, which I made to myself at the very first of the ministry, apply in a large degree to the ministry of the present time.

(1) I will begin my pastorate with an unquestioning faith in Jesus Christ as the one and only power in all of the world, and the only one capable of saving the world. I will define my Christ as the greatest Statesman and Economist of all time, and insist that legislation and education and political

189

economy and industry look to Him as the one in all the world as holding in His teaching the redemption of the world at every point. He is not a Redeemer unless He is a Statesman, for man to be fully redeemed, he must be redeemed socially, politically, economically, as well as theologically. Think on this: If men sought first the kingdom of God through Jesus Christ, they would have all the other material things necessary for human happiness.

(2) I will, so far as lies in my power, begin my ministry by loving my people. Many ministers fail to have a genuine affection for all sorts and conditions of men. If I do not really have a feeling of compassion and regard for every person in my parish, there is something fatal in my ministry.

(3) I will spend much time in prayer—a habit I learned as a child in the Dakota Territory. Furthermore, I will never be too busy to find time for prayer. I will pray alone and with groups of my people in their homes. And I will allow nothing to interfere with a period of prayer on Sunday morning or evening just before the preaching services. During those times I will shut the door on all other matters, and with a chosen few of the spiritually minded in my church family we will pray for the divine blessing on the message of the day.

That said, looking back, I would change many habits connected with prayer life. I would use the Sunday morning service often for a prayer service as I have come to believe that in the American pulpit there is far too much preaching and too little praying. I would, without previous notice, on some Sunday mornings when the church was filled with people who had heard preaching ever since they were born, lay my sermon aside, tell the organist not to play or the choir to sing, give out no notices, leave the morning offering to be given as the people went out, and say to the people, "Prayer is the Christian's vital breath. Therefore let us spend this gracious hour in prayer." And I have faith enough to believe that if that were done spontaneously in every pulpit in America, not once or twice but often, possibly limiting the preaching of sermons to once a month, we would be having the greatest revival in the history of the church.

(4) I will emphasize the work of the preacher as teacher instead of orator and speaker. I would be the first to admit that I am not a great orator, and that my preaching style is more like having a conversation. Even if I were known for my public speaking ability, I believe I would still advocate teaching as one

191

of the pastor's primary responsibilities. For Central Church, that meant turning the morning preaching service into a teaching period for several months in the year. It meant having the Bible School condense its time into forty minutes and then coming into the church auditorium for the eleven o'clock service. Then with all classes seated with their teachers or department superintendents, we would have an hour or more of a religious service using the stately hymns of the church, and teaching instead of preaching. The end and aim of all the services was to reach decisions to live the Christian life, join the Church, and begin to be a disciple.

(5) I will try to do in between two Sundays the most important part of my ministry. I will ask my people to free me from formal pastoral calls, and let me use my time and strength in calling on the sick, the shut-ins, and the afflicted. If the people cannot trust me to use my time in the best ways, they had better never have called me to be their pastor. In accordance with this plan, I will write many letters to my men, not letters of complaint or criticism or fault-finding, but letters of commendation and of Christian cheer. I will also spend a good part of every day out of doors instead of in a close study room.

(6) I will make it my business to know the Bible better than any man in my congregation. And when it comes to reading books, I will read only those that minister to life. There are not many such books so it happens that in the course of the years, my library is small. But that is fine with me because the Bible contains the entire story of man's need, of his develop-ment, of his sinning and his redemption, and his future. May I be allowed to express my heretical views on the habit of book reading indulged in by many ministers. There are hun-dreds of ministers in our churches whose ser-mons are nothing but diluted reviews of diluted books. The years go by and the one great source of wisdom for the preacher—the Bible—is neglected while he pays his hard-won coin for books that do not nourish the heart or stimulate the mind.

(7) I will take the greatest possible care of my body in order to preserve for my people and the calling to which I am called, a well-governed machine, not liable to break down or wear out before its usefulness is exhausted. A minister, as I have written at least once, must be made of cast iron and firebrick in order to stand the wear of these times. Thus, I have found that a good horseshoe game every after-noon with a neighbor has been worth more to

me than golf or walking, and the expense is only nominal. In any case, the minister of all men needs to keep his body in shape, for the strain is enormous and he needs, if any man does, a physical endurance that will prevent depression, and at the same time be a constant example to his own people of Christian strength. In the same vein, the Christian ministry need not be afraid to teach the healing power of God on the body through prayer. I believe that the minister of today has as much right to pray for recovery of the sick in his parish as any minister in Paul's time or in the early centuries of the history of the church.

(8) I will set apart a regular time and consecrate it to the needs of any human being in the parish for the confessional of the soul's needs. By this I mean what I tried to carry out for many years in the establishment of a Sunday afternoon period, which I called the "Open Door," when any one in the parish who wanted to confess his need could come to the church study and find an opportunity to give his soul's or mind's or body's need the relief of telling it to the minister with the hope of receiving help. I believe one of the greatest sources of the Protestant church power is being missed because we do not open a door of hope to the people in our parishes. This is

not a confessional where the minister stands like a priest between the soul and his divine need of forgiveness for sin, but a confessional where the minister meets the people of his parish who are in trouble and offers them his human help and prayers. I can think of nothing that remains with me as a source of joy of heart like those hours spent with troubled souls that came and broke down the stony walls of custom and isolation and revealed the hunger they had carried for long years in their desire to tell to another the heartache or the fear or the need that could not be told to any one but the minister. While many of these sessions were without the relief of an immediate answer, none of them was useless. In a host of cases the pastor's study became a place of glorious light breaking into a lifetime of terrible darkness, and those who came into the little room with fear and trembling went away with smiles of hope and new faces shining through the rainbows of their tears.

(9) Finally, I pledged myself at the very beginning of my ministry that no matter what happened in my local parish or anywhere out in the great world I would never lose my faith in the ultimate victory of the things that Jesus lived and died for. If my ministry could not carry with it always the impression of beating

*the devil and saving the world, I had no call to
be a minister. I am glad to say I have never
doubted the final victory of good over evil. If I
could not preach and teach a Christ Who could
and would draw all men up unto Himself, I had
no Christ to preach worth talking about.*

*Friend, if I were beginning life again I do
not know of any place where I would prefer to
begin than in the ministry. But whatever you
choose to do with your life, love God and obey
Him. Envy not the rich. True happiness consists in a conscience at peace with God and a
heart free from selfish desires and habits. In
spite of the many obstacles the world through
the devil throws in your path, take heart in the
words of our Lord Jesus Christ, words that I
have repeated to myself countless times over
the years: "Be of good cheer. I have overcome
the world."*

Yours in Christ,
Charles M. Sheldon

Until his retirement from the ministry, the biggest
question of his life had been the now familiar query,
What would Jesus do? Now he was faced with the
more difficult question: What would Charles Sheldon
do? While he had been a devoted husband and father,
he admittedly had not spent much time with May and

Merriam. Years earlier, he had plumbed his own feelings of inadequacy as a husband and father in the pages of *Robert Hardy's Seven Days:*

> *Ah! Fathers and husbands, you who are toiling for the dear ones at home, how many of you have grown so unaccustomed to the tender affections of home that your own wife would almost faint and think something was going to happen to you if you kissed her good-bye when you went away to your work in the morning! How do you know that she who has been your faithful friend and lover all these years, and nursed you through peevish sickness and done a thousand things every day for you without so much as a word of thanks or praise on your part—how do you know she does not care for these demonstrations of affection? And if she does not, how does it happen, except through neglect?*

May had understood the depth of his commitment to the ministry almost from the moment she met Charles. But Merriam, born the very year of his father's greatest success, would not be so pliable. Perhaps rebelling against his father's pristine reputation or acting as the stereotypical "preacher's kid," he would leave home for good after graduation from high school. A disappointment to his father, Merriam did not hesitate to smoke or drink liquor in Charles's presence, an eerie reminder of several characters in Charles's earliest novels. He did join the family occasionally for summer outings at their cabin on Crystal Lake near Frankfort, Michigan, but he kept his distance for the most part. As an adult, Merriam pursued a career in banking, like his maternal grandfather, eventually marrying and having children of his own. Sadly, though, following a long illness, Merriam Sheldon would commit suicide twenty years or so after his father's death.

While he could not make up for the lost years, Charles nonetheless began to be more of a homebody, spending hours with May in pursuit of their hobbies and entertaining friends, especially those who were lonely and in need of cheering up. Throughout her life, and now into Charles's retirement, May had enjoyed playing the piano and being involved in the local theater. She had tried her hand at acting and directing, and now she began dramatizing several of Charles's Sunday evening novels. Charles continued his own writing, penning his autobiography and other novels. It wasn't long before he received a most enticing offer from a publication he had always supported.

In January 1920 Charles was asked to become editor-in-chief of the *Christian Herald,* the same periodical whose ads had been proudly displayed in the Sheldon Edition of the Topeka *Daily Capital.* A friend to many at the Herald, Charles was especially close to Daniel A. Poling, who had served with him on the Flying

Squadron. He would be required to contribute a weekly column to the publication as well as make five or six trips to New York during the year for administrative meetings. He would make good use of the thirty-six-hour train ride from Kansas to New York, as he spent much of it answering the more than three hundred letters he received each week.

Never once did he entertain the notion of moving to New York, as many expected him to do. Kansas was where he would remain. "For I believe I can truly say," he wrote a few years later, "that the spot where a man has been married, and where his son has been born, and where he has preached for more than a quarter of a century—the spot where he has baptized little children, and welcomed disciples into the Communion, and performed the marriage ceremony over two thousand times, where he has stood with families over their dead, and watched young life grow upward into gracious manhood and womanhood, yes. . .is dearer to him than any other spot, and that is my feeling toward Kansas, where the prairie wind softly blowing in the clean air on a May morning brings to my open study window the perfect notes of the meadow lark, and gives me inspiration for a better world."

In 1925, tired at last of those train rides, Charles gave up his largely figurehead position and was promptly given the new title of contributing editor, a position he would hold until his death.

Financially, Charles and May would be fairly well

off in their retirement years. Although Charles had never made more than $2,500 per year at Central Church and never gave much thought to money in general, May (and May alone) had inherited her parents' entire estate, leaving the couple quite comfortable. (The terms of Everet Merriam's will were very specific; the wise banker had known both his son-in-law's strengths and his weaknesses.) For one thing, they were able to sell their home on 15th Street and move into the Merriams' more spacious home near Washburn College (on College Street). While May held the purse strings, she did indulge her husband his love of travel, and the two embarked on several trips, including an adventure sailing to the Holy Land in 1926, a trip sponsored by *Christian Herald*.

There, in the land then known as Palestine, Charles finally had the opportunity to walk in Jesus' steps. He sat on the ancient curbing around Jacob's Well where Jesus was said to have confronted the Samaritan woman with her past. He also preached on Mt. Carmel, the Mount of Olives, and Mars Hill in Athens, Greece, and from the shores of the Sea of Galilee. To sit where his Master had once sat, to walk the dusty roads, to gaze out at the countryside of His youth were experiences that would be etched in Charles's soul. He had lived a life fuller than most, and he had capped his journey with what, to him, was the ultimate experience.

twelve

Topeka, Kansas, January 1946

The day had somehow escaped him. He had drifted off to sleep, a common occurrence, and now he saw through the window all that remained of the fleeting light of day. May was probably checking on him now, rubbing her fingers on the frosted panes of glass to catch the first sign of life emerging from the brown study. He wouldn't disappoint her; he'd be home soon for an early supper.

On his desk he had set aside an announcement from last Sunday's church bulletin, one that he wanted to keep. The announcement was a reminder to the congregation to set aside February 26, Charles's eighty-ninth birthday, for an unusual ceremony. He knew he was absentminded—he had recently left May in a gasoline station restroom and taken off in the car alone—but he couldn't forget his own birthday. Or could he? Well, May would have to remind him again. That day would mark the burning of the mortgage on the new Sheldon Community House, an occasion he hoped he would live to see. After all, he didn't want to get to heaven knowing that a building that bore his name was still in debt. He laughed out loud at the thought. This coming from the man who never knew how many coins he had in his pocket!

The Sheldon Community House, which was an addition to Central Church, had been a gift to Charles upon his retirement from the congregation, though it took a few years to get the project off and running. After preparations to raise funds for the $100,000 structure began in 1922, ground was at last broken in early 1924 and the building was officially dedicated in November 1924.

Whenever he thought of this lasting tribute to his ministry, tears came to his eyes. He loved walking inside the Community House, loved hearing all the laughter and running and playing going on there. The building was large enough to accommodate a gymnasium, classrooms, library, chapel, and theater—with rooms to spare for other uses. Yes, he would be there for this final ceremony, God willing.

As he looked at the familiar piles atop his desk, he realized he had accomplished little this day. Shaking his head to clear the cobwebs, he remembered he had been rereading "Two Old Friends: Old Age and Death," one of his favorite stories, before he drifted off to sleep. What particular passage had he been looking for when sleep so rudely overcame him? His shaking index finger, moving up and down the columns, suddenly stopped and tapped the site with an air of success. He put on his spectacles and read aloud:

> *There are no lonesome hearthstones for those who have been wise enough to look ahead to the time when riches, honors, office, fame, take on their proper value and friends are welcomed in to take the places once given to ambition and love of applause, and worldly success. The Master was a young man. But He spoke the rich experience of the Man of the ages when one day he said to His disciples, "No longer do I call you servants, but friends."*

Clumsily, he pulled on his galoshes and slowly buttoned his overcoat for the trek home. Then he sat for a moment before facing the cold blast of the north wind. *One day, very soon, I will no longer walk in His steps. Perhaps in heaven we can walk side by side.*

A few days later, upon returning from the brown study, Charles was surprised to see May dressed in her finery, as if she planned to go out for the evening. A smile tugged at her mouth and her eyes twinkled as she looked at her confused husband.

"Just say you don't remember," she said teasingly.

"Today is not my birthday, I know that at least," he retorted.

"Your new suit is freshly pressed and on the bed. We have to be at the theater at seven sharp, Charles."

Theater, theater, he thought. *Ah yes, perhaps I didn't want to remember after all. Tonight promises to be a very long evening.* The Women's Club of Topeka was putting on what was billed as a "Historical Pageant of Kansas," and rumor had it the production was at least four hours long. He would go, albeit reluctantly, for May's sake.

More than four hours later, after periods of intermittent dozing, Charles rose from his seat in the theater, stiffer than he had felt in a while. He helped May with her coat and then put his own on, while inching his way down the aisle to the exit. As they reached the long flight of stairs from the balcony to the street level, Charles attempted to grab the railing, but somehow never found it in time. When his knees refused to bend, he went crashing down the steps, landing in a crumpled heap at the bottom. There were screams and cries for help, but he heard none of them.

The next thing he knew, he was in the hospital. May was there, alongside the doctor, telling him he was fortunate to be alive, and he believed her.

He would go home soon to recuperate, a little warier of venturing outside than before. Stairs weren't so much of a problem, but he was afraid of falling on the ice and maybe breaking something that wouldn't heal so quickly.

A few weeks later, on February 18, he was pleased to receive some visitors from Central Church. Sitting in his rocking chair, Charles rocked back and forth as they discussed the plans they were making for his birthday and the burning of the mortgage.

"May will make sure I get there," he said as he stood to show his guests to the door. But after a few steps, he fell to the floor, unconscious. He had apparently collapsed from a stroke, brought on most likely from the trauma of his fall. Again he was taken to the hospital, but this time he would not return to the house on College Street. Charles Sheldon died peacefully six days later, on Sunday evening, February 24, 1946, two days before his eighty-ninth birthday.

Flags atop the state capitol and city hall were flown at half-mast the day of the funeral. But that somber reminder would be in stark contrast to the actual funeral. It seemed that the whole town of Topeka had turned out for the service, which was held on his birthday. Charles had requested a joyous ceremony, and he would have been pleased with the result. There were readings from "Two Old Friends: Old Age and Death," recitations of Charles's written prayers, and tributes to the man who had spent his life walking in His steps. The service ended, as Charles had instructed, with the "Hallelujah Chorus" from Handel's *Messiah*.

In an editorial in the *Christian Herald,* editor Daniel

A. Poling offered these words of farewell. When explaining why Charles Sheldon was the most popular contributor to the publication, he wrote, "Well, I think it was because he, more than any other man, wrote from the heart of things and persons, to the hearts of men, women, and little children. Dr. Sheldon lived 'in a house by the side of the road,' but he lived also for all houses that were set in humble places. He saw their dwellers with kindly eye while he smote the evils that exploited them." Under the veneer of life experience and fame was still the young boy who had learned to survive on the prairie, and the young man who found a way to sprinkle water on Main Street.

Decades later, a best-selling book, not to mention "WWJD" paraphernalia, defines his legacy. But to those who seek to know the man who was Charles Monroe Sheldon, Scripture is more fitting:

> *For I was an hungred, and ye gave me meat: I was thirsty, and ye gave me drink: I was a stranger, and ye took me in: Naked, and ye clothed me: I was sick, and ye visited me: I was in prison, and ye came unto me. And the King shall answer and say unto them, Verily I say unto you, Inasmuch as ye have done it unto one of the least of these my brethren, ye have done it unto me.*
>
> Matthew 25:35–36, 40

In other words, Charles Sheldon walked in His steps.

HEROES OF THE FAITH

This exciting biographical series explores the lives of famous Christian men and women throughout the ages. These trade paper books will inspire and encourage you to follow the example of these "Heroes of the Faith" who made Christ the center of their existence. 208 pages each. Only $3.97 each!